RACE AND THE SENSES

SENSORY STUDIES SERIES

Series Editor: David Howes

As the leading publisher of scholarship on the culture of the senses, we are delighted to present this series of cutting-edge case studies, syntheses and translations in the emergent field of sensory studies. Building on the success of the *Sensory Formations* series, this new venture provides an invaluable resource for those involved in researching and teaching courses on the senses as subjects of study and means of inquiry. Embracing the insights of a wide array of humanities and social science disciplines, the field of sensory studies has emerged as the most comprehensive and dynamic framework yet for making sense of human experience. The series offers something for every disciplinary taste and sensory inclination.

RACE AND THE SENSES

The Felt Politics of Racial Embodiment

SACHI SEKIMOTO AND CHRISTOPHER BROWN

Routledge
Taylor & Francis Group

LONDON AND NEW YORK

First published 2020 by Bloomsbury Academic

2 Park Square, Milton Park, Abingdon, Oxon OX14 4RN
605 Third Avenue, New York, NY 10017

Routledge is an imprint of the Taylor & Francis Group, an informa business

First issued in paperback 2022

Cover design: Ben Anslow
Cover image: Bird Feather (© Simon Gakhar/Getty Images)

Publisher's Note
The publisher has gone to great lengths to ensure the quality of this reprint
but points out that some imperfections in the original copies may be apparent.

A catalogue record for this book is available from the British Library.

A catalog record for this book is available from the Library of Congress.

Series: Sensory Studies Series
Typeset by Deanta Global Publishing Services, Chennai, India

ISBN 13: 978-1-350-08753-8 (hbk)
ISBN 13: 978-1-03-233690-9 (pbk)
DOI: 10.4324/9781003086499

For Taisei
Our sensory delight

CONTENTS

ACKNOWLEDGMENTS

We thank our family and friends in Japan and the United States who nurtured us throughout the process of writing this book. We appreciate the continued support from our parents, Kazue and Toshiro Sekimoto, and Louise and Hooker Brown. This book project evolved through many conversations with our friends and colleagues, including Kathryn Sorrells, John (Jack) Condon, Kyoko Kataoka, Takahiro Yamamoto, Godfried Asante, Shinsuke Eguchi, Yusaku Yajima, Osei Appiah, Timothy Berry, and Karma Chávez. We also thank Sarah Olson for writing an article on our book for the university magazine.

We developed and wrote the bulk of this book during our sabbatical leave in Japan in 2017–18. We thank our colleagues in the Department of Communication Studies and Dean Matthew Cecil for institutional and academic support for completing this book. We are deeply indebted to Tetsuya Kono at Rikkyo University in Tokyo and Chie Torigoe at Seinan Gakuin University in Fukuoka for hosting us as visiting scholars in Japan. We were able to develop our chapters by presenting at various academic outlets, including a workshop at SIETAR Japan, various symposiums organized by researchers in the Face-Body Studies, and seminars at Rikkyo University and Seinan Gakuin University. We also thank the Rhetoric, Media and Social Change Speaker Series at Drake University for giving us the opportunity to present our work. Outside of academic support, Keiko Kitagawa, Natsumi Nigawara, Ikuko Tashiro, Makiko Otaki, and Norikazu Otaki shared invaluable friendship during our stay in Japan.

We thank undergraduate and graduate students in Advanced Intercultural Communication and Race and Communication for their insights and feedback. Special thanks to Katie Olson for sharing our excitement for the book and assisting us by proofreading the manuscript. The original version of

Chapter 5 was published in *Departures in Critical Qualitative Research* in 2016 and portions of Chapters 1 and 2 were published in *Critical Philosophy of Race* in 2018. We thank the editors and reviewers of these journals for helping us pave the path toward this book project.

We thank David Howes, the series editor, for the opportunity to explore our inquiry on race and the senses on our terms and in our creative and intellectual capacity. We also thank the anonymous reviewers for their suggestions and feedback. We are grateful for the incredible editorial and production team at Bloomsbury Academic for their support and dedication, including Miriam Cantwell, Lucy Carroll, Lily McMahon, Angelique Neumann, and Rennie Alphonsa.

Our deepest appreciation goes to our son, Taisei, for shining our way forward and giving us the reason to embrace our senses fully.

1

Introduction

Feeling Race

Race and the Senses elaborates on the following argument: race is felt and sensed into being. Multiple senses are engaged to *feel* race and racial differences, and such embodied multisensory feelings are integral to the social, political, and ideological construction of race. We wrote this book as a form of somatic work,[1] in which we engaged our own senses and examined our lived sensations to question, describe, and reveal the social sensorium infused with racial meanings and racialized ways of feeling. That is, the senses are both the object of our investigation and the means of our inquiry. Grounded in the authors' bodily and sensorial experiences as a Japanese woman living in the United States (Sachi) and an African American man from Chicago (Chris), each chapter explores the lived sensations of racism and racialization by investigating how race appeals to and is entangled with our lived and sensorial embodiment. As coauthors and life partners, we explore the world of race as a multisensorial event, paying attention to how race is constructed, reproduced, and experienced *feelingly* through our sensory perceptions, affective engagements, and embodied experiences.

Our inquiry into the relationships between race and the senses are driven by two primary purposes. First, while race as a visual construct has long informed and shaped the public and scholarly discussions on race, this book expands the scope of racial theorizing by attending to the multisensory dimensions of race, racialization, and racism. The visual dimension of racial experience is pervasive and undeniable: race functions as a visual economy of difference in which visible phenotypes are coded into hierarchical social relations. Visual perception of race, however, is always intertwined with other sensory, affective, and emotional experiences. Not only do we see race, we interact with its various sensations somatically. We explore how race is not only seen but also felt and registered through multiple and intertwined senses and sensations. Second, we explore the possibility of using embodied experiences and bodily sensations as a source of knowledge. The lived body is both an affective medium of subjective experience and a site where power relations and ideological norms are habituated. We examine bodily sensations and visceral feelings to reveal and problematize how social norms, values, and relations of power are habituated and materialized into lived embodiment.

As we examine the relationship between race and the senses, we seek epistemological possibilities in the realm of feeling. By "feeling," we do not simply mean emotions, but all-encompassing sensations experienced through somatic, affective, and sensorial engagements in the world. Our approach resonates with theories of embodied epistemology such as the "somatic mode of attention" advanced by Thomas J. Csordas and consciousness as "feeling in the body" as delineated by Kathryn Linn Geurts.[2] Knowledge is always more than properties in the mind, and the act of knowing is a full-body experience. We use "feeling" interchangeably with "sensing." The emphasis on feeling shifts our focus from the rationalistic head to the whole body as a location and instrument of knowledge construction. The act of feeling is an ongoing phenomenon that surrounds or envelops our bodies as we gauge our presence in the world. Thus, we write not only *about* the senses but also *through* the senses.

The focus on the felt dimensions of race and racism does not mean we can simply replace the critique of symbolic representation, ideological discourses, and institutional construction of race. Rather, the point is to expand the scope of critique to encompass not only the visible (language, discourse, or mental categories) but also the invisible or pre-reflective dimensions of racialized realities (the flows, movements, sensations, and sensuous qualities). Our goal is not to make a totalizing or universal claim about race and sensory experience, nor is it our purpose to essentialize sensory experiences of racial groups or identity. Instead, we sensorialize the inquiry into race to give a fuller, more materially grounded and embodied account of race. In our approach, race is not merely an inorganic "construct," "system," or "structure" of oppression, but rather an assemblage of sensuous realities with texture, movement, rhythm, temperature, and weight. Race materializes as a bodily, affective, and sensorial *event*—something that *happens*, rather than something that *is*—that involves ongoing and emergent entanglements of feeling subjects, lived sensations, symbolic interpretations, and discursive/institutional structure.[3]

The point is not about revealing the falsity of race as a construction, but about how the invented idea gains traction to become and continue to be real in our lived experiences. The mantra of "race is socially constructed" fails to capture seemingly more intuitive and commonsensical perceptions of racial differences. The statement "just because race is socially constructed, doesn't mean it's not real" is rather misleading.[4] Perhaps a more accurate statement is this: "Race is real *because* it is socially (and perceptually) constructed." The realness of race is more often implicitly felt and held true without being brought into conscious awareness or logical analysis. Race continues to be one of the most hegemonic constructs in modern history precisely because it is "registered feelingly."[5] What we need is not to convince ourselves how race is not *really* real, but to unpack the processes and mechanisms through which race has become real, perceptually, materially, and experientially.

In the following, we first situate our inquiry within the growing and multidisciplinary efforts to study race and racism from sensory, sensorial, and phenomenological perspectives. Second, we lay out our theoretical perspective that foregrounds *feeling* as a modality of phenomenological investigation grounded in embodied sensory experiences. Third, we conceptualize the body as a sensuous subject, followed by a discussion of the interrelationships between culture, power, and the senses. Finally, we conclude by addressing our methodological orientation and previewing the upcoming chapters.

The Sensory Turn in the Scholarship of Race and Racism

As a multidisciplinary effort, the sensory turn in social sciences and humanities articulates and accounts for the dynamic and complex interrelationships between culture and the senses.[6] Extending the sensory perspectives into studying race, various scholars have contributed to this emergent and growing body of knowledge by foregrounding the senses as the medium through which racial worlds are constructed and experienced. For example, scholars have investigated the historical construction of race through the notion of sensory stereotypes;[7] the role of vision in the perception and attribution of racial differences;[8] the racialization of vision through the use of images and photographs;[9] the resistive performance of "loud black girls" in high school;[10] the racialized performativity of black female loudness and Asian male quietness;[11] the acoustic space of whiteness;[12] the racialization of voice, accent, and music;[13] the racialized modes of listening;[14] the racialized scents of urban migrant communities;[15] the interconnection between the visual and the tactile in intercultural cinema;[16] the sensory construction of multicultural urban space in the food market;[17] the intersection between racial identity and food culture;[18] and the theoretical articulation of the sensory apparatus of race.[19] These scholarly contributions demonstrate the role of the senses in constructing, mediating, performing, and materializing race.

In addition to anthropological and sociological studies of race and the senses, philosophical and phenomenological analyses of race and racial embodiment have made significant contributions by foregrounding the lived body as a locus of critical theorizing. Our sensory exploration into race is theoretically informed and inspired by the phenomenological writings of Frantz Fanon; Linda Martín Alcoff's articulation of racial embodiment; Sara Ahmed's theorizing of phenomenology of racialized identity and whiteness; Iris Marion Young's critique of gendered embodiment and spatiality; George Yancy's account of how the white objectifying gaze surveils and oppresses black bodies[20] and Arun Saldanha's ontological approach to race.[21] In recent years, scholars such as Emily S. Lee and Helen Ngo have provided critical phenomenological articulations of racial embodiment, demonstrating the significance of understanding race through the lived body.[22] Encompassing multiple scholarly disciplines, the scholarship on the interconnections of race, embodiment, and the senses reflects the growing interest in articulating the sensuous existence of race as something material, visceral, and habituated.

In *Race and the Senses*, we use theoretical insights from phenomenology to foreground lived embodiment, while also tapping into the reservoir of knowledge from sensory studies to emphasize that the body is not simply about what it *is* or what it *does*, but more fundamentally about what and how it *feels*. The body feels as it moves, touches, tastes, hears, smells, dances, sweats, and aches. The body also feels other bodies, and senses other animate and non-animate beings. When it comes to race—and other social identifiers of differences—the body is not merely an object on which racial differences are inscribed, but it is simultaneously the subject that feels such inscription. This book explores the sensuous materiality of race by examining how racialized bodies feel race, racialization, and racial embodiment. While phenomenology allows us to explore lived experience as embodied, research in sensory studies reminds us to attend to the specificity of the sensorial world as culturally coded and socially cultivated.

The sensorial and phenomenological approach allows us to address some of the limitations of the prevailing approach to studying race. In her critique of the social constructionist approach to gender, Asia Friedman aptly points out its limitation to truly challenge what people perceive to be "natural" about gender differences: "Although critically important in the feminist movement, the idea that gender is socially constructed has not been able to erase in most people's minds what seem like 'natural' differences between men and women, and attacks on the idea that gender is socially constructed continue."[23] The same critique must be applied to those devoted to theorizing or analyzing the social construction of race. Although critically important in the anti-racist movement, the idea that race is socially constructed has not been able to erase in most people's minds what seem like "natural" differences between races. Friedman argues that the sensory perception is an integral part of the mechanism of social construction of reality: "Reality is experienced—and fundamentally shaped—through our senses. It is only via the senses that the world enters our minds and our experience, and sensing the world is a way of building and reshaping the way the world is assembled."[24] Similarly, David Howes emphasizes the primacy of sensory experience as "an arena for structuring social roles and interactions. We learn social divisions, distinctions of gender, class, and race, through our senses," and therefore "sensual relations are social relations."[25]

The prevailing social constructionist approach that privileges the cognitive and intellectualist intervention often fails to address the deeply embedded racial feelings and racialized habits. David A. Granger asserts that a restricted faith on "right thinking approaches" to challenge racial intolerance and enmity oftentimes has repercussions of revitalizing discursive logics of the mind-body dualisms.[26] The current backlash of white racial grievances and more explicit display of white nationalism can be understood as an outcome of the suppressed racist bodily feelings and habits in the name of post-racial society and racial colorblindness. The visceral grip of racism cannot simply be resolved by the logic of postracialism or liberal multiculturalism. The critique of structural racism often results in disembodying issues of race by locating the problem in the inorganic institutions and structures rather than in lived bodies and minds that abide by such institutions and structures. Racial encounters are never completely cognitive or purely institutional. As Friedman argues, race is a social accomplishment—it involves lived, embodied subjects who act, move, feel, think, and experience race with varying degrees of agency and awareness.[27] Race is not a static object that circulates within social discourse and practice; race is charged with emotion, affective energy, communal affiliation, moral orientation, gut reaction, bodily rhythms, and multisensorial memories. Race, racism, and racial relations all manifest and morph within the intersecting web of intersubjective sensorial experiences.

Rather than focusing on deconstructing the constructed nature of social reality, we focus on the multisensory and intersensorial conditions in which the invented idea of race becomes sensible and *feel-able*. Race, at its core, is an idea that provokes our bodily, sensory, affective, and emotional engagement.[28] Once it is socially and ideologically activated, the idea of race holds grip on our bodies and psyches.[29] In this book, we bring into focus various ways in which we come to *know* race, seemingly intuitively and commonsensically, through our bodily, sensorial, and affective encounters with others. We believe how we *feel* race—rather than feel *about* race—is the elephant in the room when it comes to talking about race. Regardless of one's political affiliation, ideological orientation, or the level of racial awareness, we all live in what Davide Panagia calls "a regime of perception" in which our perceptual attention and bodily awareness are cultivated and oriented according to racial meanings and hierarchies.[30] This book examines the instances and processes through which a regime of racial perception becomes embodied—that is, become part of our bodily habits and perceptual subjectivity—beyond, beneath, or alongside our conscious awareness. Race is felt and sensed by lived and sentient subjects, rather than constructed by an anonymous social force or contained exclusively within individual minds. Thus, we examine the sensuousness of racialized social worlds as not only *constructed* but also materially, viscerally, and experientially *felt*. In what follows, we elaborate on our theoretical perspective that foregrounds feeling as a somatic modality of knowing.

The Epistemology of Feeling

By focusing on what we call the *epistemology of feeling*, we bring attention to lived experiences of feeling as a means of critical inquiry. In the Western paradigm of mind-body dualism, there is a deep divide between the act of thinking (rational, logical, and conceptual) and the experience of feeling (irrational, ambiguous, and transient). We contend that the divide between thinking and feeling is conceptually convenient but phenomenologically inaccurate: "Humans *can* know, sense, and thus craft meaning carnally, without the necessary aid of abstract symbols."[31] The act of thinking—what surfaces as an explicit linguistic articulation of idea—is always supported and substantiated by various sensorial experiences that remain unarticulated or implicit. That is, "Sense experience operates at the membrane between the sensible and the thinkable."[32]

Alexis Shotwell points out that in contrast with propositional knowledge (i.e., knowledge that is verbalized, explicit, and articulated), implicit understanding is a form of knowing that is felt through the body, but remains unarticulated. Various forms of implicit understanding—practical, somatic, and affective—provide "the conditions for things to make sense to us."[33] The social construction of race, then, is the construction of a social apparatus in which race becomes commonsensical not only through explicit thinking but also through implicit feeling: "Racialization, racism, and racial formation involve significant implicit understandings; the nonpropositional is important to forming the background of 'race.'"[34] Racial stereotypes or racist worldviews seem commonsensical for some people not because they are logically coherent, but because they resonate with their implicit, felt understanding of the nature of social difference and hierarchy. In this case, what matters in the maintenance of racialized society is its somatic and affective resonance over logic or reason, as "feelings, implicit prejudices, and bodily responses constitute a significant part of racial formation itself."[35]

To seek knowledge in the multisensorial ways of feeling is to pay attention to felt bodily sensations as a manifestation of repeated social practices that are sedimented into the body. Bodily sensations are "impressions" made on the body through social forces and interactions. We attend to such sedimented sensations and routinized impressions as sources of knowledge about race and racism. Seeking knowledge in bodily sensations and feelings means to assume that visceral sensations themselves actively produce meaning. For example, Gordon Waitt argues visceral sensations of sweat actively constitute women's gendered subjectivity, whereas Rachel Spronk claims bodily sensations of sexual pleasure substantiate social knowledge about sexuality, identity, and gender.[36] That is, bodily sensations—such as bodily sweat and erotic pleasure—don't passively wait for discursive inscription of meaning, but rather they actively materialize and give substance to the subjective interpretation of one's reality. The living, feeling body actively participates in meaning-making, rather than passively receiving meaning through the work of discourse.

Our analysis of racialized experiences is driven by the following premises: (a) we know more than we think we know, often in the form of somatic, affective, and implicit knowing/feeling; (b) our senses are intermingled within our bodily experience; and (c) our sensorial experiences are intersubjectively and intercorporeally formed and experienced with others. In the first premise, we draw attention to bodily feelings and sensations that would otherwise escape our critical analysis by unfolding the kind of knowledge embedded in the way the bodies feel and are cultivated to feel in the racialized society. In the second premise, our analysis of lived experiences of race and racism takes a multisensorial perspective, assuming that multiple senses simultaneously—if not evenly or proportionately—constitute lived experiences of racialized subjects. Fiona Newell and Ladan Shams argue that "our phenomenological experience is not of disjointed sensory sensations but is instead of a coherent multisensory world, where sounds, smells, tastes, sights, and touches amalgamate."[37] Our analysis will show how multiple sensory perceptions cohere into a felt experience in a specific context. We challenge the predominance of vision not by bringing other senses to an equal or higher status than vision, but by interrogating the intersensorial nature of social experiences and human interactions. In this case, social reality is experienced as multiple sensory modalities intermingle and co-constitute lived experiences. In the final premise, we emphasize the social dimensions of sensory engagements in which social subjects coordinate or negotiate their sensory experiences with others collectively.

The Body as a Sensuous Subject

To theorize the body as an anchor of sensory knowing of race and racism, we reject the idea that the body is only meaningful insofar as meaning is given to it through social, historical, and ideological processes. The body is not simply a passive object waiting for social signification and racist stereotyping. The body is itself, always, a sentient being that actively and continuously feels its presence, moves through social and cultural spaces, and interacts with other lived bodies.[38] As Jan Slaby contends, "The 'lived body' is the body insofar as it is the vehicle of experience of the world. It is the structure-giving background of experience, the emphatic standpoint of the subject of experience and the background of all her comportments."[39] In this case, the body itself is an intentional and a mindful condition of what makes the world knowable. This perspective assumes that the body is a productive mechanism of power whose dis/ability enables a certain kind of knowledge, experience, and meaning. There is intentionality that springs from the living body which seeks information to orient itself in the physical/social worlds, and to generate meaning through bodily awareness and experiences. The body-as-sentient approach places a greater emphasis on the sensorial and perceptual experiences of bodies to make the world meaningful. Racism, at its core, is powerful not because of the *meaning* ascribed to racialized bodies, but because it denies or subordinates the sensuous materiality of lived bodies of color.

George Lakoff and Mark Johnson explore the bodily origin of meaning by focusing on the conceptual metaphor.[40] They examine how we understand the meaning of abstract concepts by drawing on our direct sensorimotor experiences of movement, space, speed, direction, and pain, among other basic bodily experiences.[41] Our understanding of abstract concepts such as happiness, time, and morality are experientially grounded in spatial orientations of up-down, in-out, and front-back, as expressed through conceptual metaphors in statements such as "I'm feeling up/I'm feeling down," "I look forward to it," and "we are upright/they are underhanded." Our conceptual reality is made meaningful through tangible experiences of our bodily structure (with front and back), mobility (up and down, forward and backward), and the senses (pain, heat, and pleasure). In arguing that abstract concepts are largely metaphorical, Lakoff and Johnson's most significant contribution is the suggestion that the *meaningfulness* of lived reality stems from direct embodied experience of reality mediated through action and observation. The source of meaning is deeper than superficial inscriptions given to a signifier, because meaning is grounded in our basic bodily and sensory experiences. In other words, abstract meaning is rooted in, and substantiated by, our direct sensorimotor experience and bodily interaction.[42] From this perspective, the involvement of our sensorimotor system, as opposed to the sophistication of our linguistic system, makes abstract ideas meaningful and keeps us in touch with external reality.[43] Thus, intersubjective experience is possible not only by sharing of meaning assigned to words but also by sharing of associative embodied experiences that make abstract concepts tangibly meaningful.

To push the sensuous approach to the body even further, we argue that social institutions—the inorganic, anonymous system that reproduces racism—are also part of the larger collective social organ that "feels" race and racism on behalf of people. If human bodies and objects are coextensive, as provocatively argued by Brian Massumi,[44] the institution prosthetically extends the human bodies that feel race and racism, while the institution extends its "feelings" onto our bodies (we elaborate on the prosthetic nature of race in Chapter 2 and 7). Focusing on the sensorial and affective dimensions of race and racism releases us from the "grid" of identity politics to capture the movement, flow, energy, and ontogenetic aspects of racial formation.[45] In *Race and the Senses*, we examine the bodily felt dimensions of race and racism by drawing on the idea that race exists, not as an independent social object, but as an assemblage of particular sensuous qualities and sensory modalities interwoven within the ecological system of social division and regulation.

To argue that the body is always already an open field or a sentient background of social experience does not mean that the body remains pure and innocent. Rather, a materialist and sensuous understanding of the body necessitates a conceptualization of the body as historically constituted and embodied. That is, the body is an ongoing process and a site of becoming. In this sense, there is no universal or transhistorical human body, but rather each one of us is a unique body-subject,[46] materializing and enacting its possibility within the broader social, historical, biological, and ideological environments. Thus far, we have alluded to the role of the body as a sentient being in constituting meaning. In what follows, we politicize the bodily senses and sensory experiences within the context of culture and power.

Culture, Power, and the Senses

What is the relationship between *the body as an active constructor of experience* and *the hegemonic relations of power* in society? This question leads us to consider the role of the senses in the formation of culture and power.[47] As one of the most fundamental dimensions of being alive and aware, the senses become the locus of our discussion because of their mediating status between "the natural" and "the cultural." As Howes critiques, "It has been customary to associate the senses with nature, whether 'innocent' or 'savage.' The senses, in this case, symbolize the antithesis of culture."[48] A critical exploration into the senses reveals the interconnection between culture and the human sensorium, thereby fundamentally questioning what is largely taken as "natural" while challenging the boundary of "culture." Shared sensory experiences are fundamental to the formation of community, as "learning to identify with a social reality includes learning to see, hear, feel, and smell that reality in roughly the same way as the people by which one is normally surrounded."[49] Furthermore, the shared sensory experience underlies the social relations of power as "the social control of perceptibility—who is seen, who is heard, whose pain is recognized—plays an essential role in establishing positions of power within society. Such control is exercised both officially and unofficially, and determines not only *who* is perceived, but also *how* they are perceived."[50]

Contrary to the common system of thought established initially by Aristotle, Geurts argues that the five-senses model is a culturally specific categorization.[51] There are cultures that use different types of sensory orders to orient themselves in social and physical worlds, such as a sense of balance and kinesthesia. Geurts claims that "sensing . . . as 'bodily ways of gathering information,' is profoundly involved with society's epistemology, the development of its cultural identity, and its forms of being-in-the-world."[52] Through her ethnographic work in southeastern Ghana, Geurts argues that a culturally specific sensory order becomes embodied by individual members of the community and that cultural identities emerge through sensory orientations cultivated through socialization. In this sense, individuals *incorporate* social values and orientations into their bodies, as the embodied sensory orientations shape and inform their social and physical experiences.[53]

It is notable that Karl Marx politicized sensory experience and defined his vision of communism as a form of sensory emancipation through the abolition of private property. Claiming that "the *forming* of the five senses is a labor of the entire history of the world down to the present," Marx was critical of the power of private property to reduce human sensory experience into that of material possession, consumption, and objectification.[54] For Marx, capitalism dehumanizes and alienates people because it reduces the richness of human senses into a one-sided "orientation to the object"[55] in which things— including humans beings—exist only insofar as they are directly possessed, used, and consumed. To become fully human, Marx argued, means to cultivate the "richness of subjective human sensibility"[56] and "sensuous consciousness"[57] to appreciate multifaceted sensory experiences and orientations to objects. He envisioned a formation of established society in which "*social* organs" are cultivated to produce "the *rich* man [sic]" who is "*profoundly endowed with all the senses.*"[58] For Marx, the relations of power shaped by economic structures are real and material insofar as they enable or inhibit particular sensory dimensions of human existence.

Far from being a neutral receptor of environmental stimuli, the senses are socially cultivated and culturally shaped. Yet, the senses cannot be fully reduced into culturally relativistic explanations. Despite cultural variations, the senses remain fundamental in shaping human conditions and making social and cultural experiences possible. More precisely, the senses are the basic, habituated, and malleable *conditions* of experience and meaning. It is this presumably universal significance of the senses in human experience that compels us to politicize our sensory participation in the operation of racial hegemony. As Marx poignantly critiqued almost a century and a half ago, the sensorial is deeply tied to what it means to be human, and therefore the question of the senses in social contexts can never be separated from the question of power.

Methodology of the Sensuous

In *Race and the Senses*, we develop somatic reflections on embodied experiences, sensations, memories, and feelings on race, racialization, and racism by using our intermingled senses and sentient flesh to guide our inquiry. Inherent in the process of dehumanization—of which racism is a prime example—is the objectification of marginalized bodies, including the bodies of color, subordinated genders, the poor, or those who are differently abled. An object is assumed to have no feelings, not just emotionally, but physically or neurologically. That is, objectified individuals are presumed to not feel, or feel less sensitively than those in the dominant group with normative sensibilities. This projection of numbness onto the senses of the Other is used to justify or ignore violence inflicted on their bodies. At the sensorial level, oppression functions by depriving individuals of their sensorial authority and ownership of their own perceptual experience. In a racist society, for example, one's skin is objectified as a signifier of racial difference (and deviance) rather than an active feeling organ. Even though racism continuously attempts to deny people of color their sentient and visceral subjectivity, it is important to remember there is always a living, sentient, feeling person who feels such objectification. Kyoo Lee illuminates the politics of feelings experienced by those who inhabit marginalized identities:

> How does it feel to inhabit the problem of social identities without having to acknowledge it? How does it feel not to feel? Who knows: such problems of social blockage and affective zoning, of the lines drawn by "color," "gender," "class," "culture," etc., so-contrasted, so-ignored, so-used, tend to be "felt" frontmost and foremost, registered feelingly first, especially by those readily sliced and shuffled by those persistent, problematic categories.[59]

Lee points out how marginalized subjects register, feelingly, the meaning of social boundaries, while such feelings remain numb or unimaginable for privileged groups.

In reflecting on various sensorial experiences of race, we begin with and return to our direct bodily sensations, memories, and experiences, not because our experiences are unique or universal, but because we want to gain insights into the phenomenological quality of what race feels like, and what it is like to be the racialized Other. We employ our own senses, sensuous memories, and somatic reflections as the primary medium of theorizing about race. We provide the "first-body" account of racialization and racism not to essentialize sensory experiences but to preserve the rawness of a feeling body. Our account of personal experience is a form of phenomenological reflection, including descriptions of visceral sensations, somatic observations, sequences of events, emotions, and thoughts on *how race happens as a sensuous event*.[60] The narratives provided in this book encompass a phenomenology of racialized sensations, body parts, movements, and feelings, rather than a phenomenology of a unified racialized subject. We are less concerned about the "I" that emerges in racially charged interactions; we are more concerned about the felt-qualities and sensations of such encounters. In other words, we are more interested in what bodies feel and do (event), rather than what bodies are (identity). As Richard Shusterman argues, the relations of power are somatically (and often unconsciously) encoded in our habituated bodies without explicit social discourse or rules.[61] Our goal is to let these habituated feelings and bodily sensations speak for themselves, to tell us more viscerally how race touches our skin, echoes in our ears, moves our bodies, colors our vision, scents the air we breathe, or tastes on our tongues. We want to let our sensuous bodies tell us the stories of how they encounter the sensuous materiality of race and racism.

The senses mediate between the body and the world, but the field of possibility is certainly not open-ended. Cultural traditions, social norms, and relations of power shape and define the parameter of sensory experience and its signification. While race is one of the most hegemonic social constructs in modern history, we do not believe our senses are simply controlled or fooled by race as a structure of domination. We foreground the sensory dimensions of racial experience precisely because the indeterminate nature of the senses leaves us with the possibility of feeling, moving, and reaching out to the world differently. There is a tension between how our senses are cultivated, dominated, and colonized by structures of power, and how our senses nonetheless remain open and intuitive as the foundation of our (inter) subjective experience. If race is a tool of racism and a mechanism of oppression, its oppressive influence certainly reaches our sensorial experiences—our sensory perceptions are distorted to uphold and maintain racial ideologies. At the same time, as an ongoing and evolving entity, the body is always more than a product of social process—it is, rather, a process of becoming. We seek a potentially humanizing outcry in our sensorial experiences, in that our sensory perceptions are always more than what the racial regime of perception attempts to foreclose.

Preview of Chapters

In Chapter 2, we theorize race as assemblages of somatosensory feelings and sensations by examining diverse ways in which race is experienced and materialized through sensuous modalities of sight, hearing, touch, taste, and smell. We use the notion of assemblage to explore how race constitutes a sensuous event with varying degrees of intensity, movement, affectivity, and sensations. The sensory exploration into the somatic experience of race reveals two important characteristics of the relationship between race and the senses. First, race functions like a prosthetic technology that augments, amplifies, or sensitizes the bodily senses and perceptions. Using various examples of how race, racialization, and racism appeal to and shape sensory experiences and perceptions, we demonstrate the prosthetic nature of race as a social object. Second, visceral sensations and bodily feelings play a crucial role in materializing the prosthetic relationship between race and the embodied senses. We use the notion of viscosity discussed by Arun Saldanha[62] to argue that racialized bodily feelings make race stick to our bodies and senses. Thus, as a viscous prosthetic technology, race works coextensively with our bodily senses, whose sensuous feelings are vital to activate and maintain its viscosity.

In Chapter 3, Sachi examines how racialization engages and deploys multiple and intertwined assemblages of senses by focusing on the face as a site of racialization. In reflecting on the experiences of becoming Asian in the United States, she searches for the truth of her racial embodiment by returning to physical memories of the strange sensations of racialization. Claiming that the body is not simply an object of social inscription, but actively feels the world, she explores how racial inscriptions and stereotypes are felt on her face. Sachi argues the face, as a multisensorial and kinesthetic entity, is an open field of intersubjective encounters, whose shape, texture, and movement are contoured through interpersonal exchange. She considers how and why racism targets the face by attending to the tactile nature of the racializing gaze, the role of haptic visuality, as well as the kinesthetic nature of spatial affordance in racialization.

In Chapter 4, Chris engages sensuous research as a way of attuning to bodily experiences by exploring the cultural and historical trope of how race and racism are felt or sensed in the everyday experiences of black people. He examines the kinesthetic feelings of race to provide insights into the intersubjective forces that move, contour, and control the black body. By providing a sensory narrative of an encounter with law enforcement, he argues that the sensorial experiences felt by the black body in encounters with racism—such as the quivering jaw, clenched fists, and disengaged eye contact—cannot be entirely theorized or understood apart from white bodies that trigger these somatosensory modes of expression. A reading of the kinesthetic feelings of race in his sensory narrative alongside an analysis of sensory assemblages highlights how people of color *must* coordinate and negotiate movements of their bodies with the movements of whites for fear that at any moment their body could be seized or taken without repercussion.

In Chapter 5, we explore the felt sensations of speaking Standard American English (SAE) as racialized subjects. Using our phenomenological reflections, we explore the performative effects of disciplining our bodies to speak SAE as a second language and dialect. Theorizing the act of speaking as habituated embodiment in cultural matrices of power and hegemony, we foreground the sensuous materiality of the tongue and interrogate how the enactive body works as a disciplinary device for normative ways of being. By examining the phenomenology of the racialized tongue, we demonstrate how racialized subjectivities are felt through the bodily sensations of *speaking-almost-white-but-not-quite*.

In Chapter 6, Chris explores the sensorial underpinnings and embodied nature of cross-racial empathy. Approaching empathy as visceral feeling-with, he recounts the face-to-face interactions with two white male elites in leadership positions who shared their experiences of racism. He describes the exchanges with them to show how telling stories about racism is accompanied by the transmission of emotional, affective, and visceral sensations from one person to another, and from one body to another body. His sensorial narrative descriptions indicate that empathetic connection is (or can be) established when there is a flow in verbal and nonverbal exchanges, whether through sharing silence, nodding the head, affirmative eye contact, engaging posture, or through general synchrony in conversational rhythm. Furthermore, emotionally charged stories about experiences of racism recall in the listener's body the sensations of pain, anger, and frustration he or she experienced before, allowing the listener to feel with the other. That is, empathy manifests not only as emotional alignment between the two but bodily and sensorial alignment as if one inhabits another's body. The chapter reveals the moments and possibilities of cross-racial empathy as well as its failures and disruptions.

In Chapter 7, we provide several pedagogical insights that emerged through our exploration into the multisensorial experiences of racial embodiment. We discuss the visceral and viscous nature of racism, the prosthetic relation between race and the senses, as well as the pedagogical utility of developing a somatic and sensorial awareness for anti-racism. We argue that the prevailing view of race as a visual construct, along with the suppression and stigmatization of racist feelings, prevents us from understanding the multisensory and coextensive relationship between social subject (the sentient body-subject) and social object (race). It is important to become aware of how race engages multiple senses and manifests in bodily feelings, rather than trying to curtail racialized perceptions or commanding the body to tune out the "gut reaction" of racist habits. If the structures of power and domination manipulate, regulate, and inhibit our sensory openness, it is through the act of critical reflective feeling and somatic learning that we may reveal, problematize, and imagine alternative ways of reaching toward one another.

2

The Visceral Is Political

Race as Sensory Assemblage

Grounded in the work of Gilles Deleuze and Félix Guattari,[1] the notion of assemblage has productively contributed to the theorizing of race and racism by shifting the focus from what race *is* to what race *does*.[2] Dan Swanton theorizes race as a technology that produces, regulates, and transforms the intensification of certain affects, emotions, and perceptions in a given social interaction.[3] Technology, in this context, is an inventive, productive, and disciplinary mechanism of social formation that catalyzes and regulates how bodies move, feel, sense, think, and interact with others to achieve particular social outcomes. Swanton argues that race is "best understood as an assemblage. As a precarious, open-ended achievement constituted through diverse relations and connections between material and conceptual elements that include skin colour, segregation, clothing, religion, colonialism, DNA, law, travel, cultural habits, sexual mores, language, migration, and fear."[4] In this case, race manifests as an assemblage of particular arrangements and intensification of these various elements.

Zeus Leonardo and Michalinos Zembylas critique whiteness as an affective technology in which particular affective attachments and detachments, inclusion and exclusion, as well as social proximity and distance are produced and maintained for and by white subjects.[5] They argue that white affectivity, such as anti-racist sentiment or white guilt, functions as an intellectual alibi of white anti-racism, while whites' fear of blackness attests to black criminality.[6] That is, how white bodies feel, not just what they think, serves to regulate discourses and practices of racism and anti-racism. White subjectivity manifests as an affective assemblage whereby bodies gather and cohere collectively to feel in certain ways.[7] Zembylas extends the theoretical utility of examining race as an affective technology by viewing embodied social interactions as constitutive of race and racialized affectivity.[8] As Jasbir Puar points out, the notion of assemblage enables us to examine the dynamic and multisensory dimensions of social phenomena: "Assemblages allow us to attune to movements, intensities, emotions, energies, affectivities, and textures as they inhabit events, spatiality, and corporealities. Intersectionality privileges naming, visuality, epistemology, representation, and meaning, while assemblage underscores feeling, tactility, ontology, affect, and information."[9]

In this chapter, we approach race as assemblages of somatosensory experience and intersubjective affectivity. Specifically, we explore how race is held together as an "event" that cumulates not only through legal discourses, cultural ideologies, and institutional practices but also through the flesh of our lived bodies. How does race cohere into a stabilized social construct as an assemblage of sensory, affective, and bodily experiences? We extend the discussion on race as a collection of affective, material, and ideological forces by theorizing race as a sensory assemblage. That is, we approach race as a prosthetic technology that augments, amplifies, or sensitizes various embodied modalities of sensing and feeling. In this sense, the bodily senses become the medium of racialization, and thus constitute sites where race is assembled as a socially feel-able object. Felt sensations then become an alibi of the realness of race—we not only think race to be real but feel its materiality, tangibility, and presence through our body. Erin Manning argues that the senses are prosthetic, supplementing and extending the dimensions of the body.[10] The senses envelop and extend our bodies toward other bodies, objects, and environments. Our bodies do not simply respond to sensory stimuli based on a predetermined function of a sensory receptor, but every sensory encounter opens up a possibility of altering the body prosthetically.

Manning posits such processes are emergent and inventive rather than dualistic and predetermined. If the senses are prosthetic, in a racist society our embodied senses are technologized to feel, move, and experience race and racial differences with a particular configuration, intensity, and arrangement of bodily sensibilities.

In their discussion on the sensorial metaphor of "society as a body," David Howes and Constance Classen point to the nature of society as a sensorial apparatus with "organic unity, interdependence and hierarchy. . . . [Society] is not, therefore, just something to think about, but something to *feel through*."[11] To conceptualize society as a body means to approach society as a collective feeling organ, as exemplified in another sensorial metaphor: "The pulse of society." Various social collectivities, such as nation-state, ethnicity, race, gender, and class, cultivate, suppress, or amplify certain ways of sensing and feeling. Howes and Classen emphasize that rather than merely "imagined," as Benedict Anderson claimed, society is deeply felt and sensed by its members.[12] The sense of belonging to a community speaks to an intersensorial and intercorporeal connectivity, producing bodies that feel responsively and harmoniously with one another. To belong to a community is to share a greater degree of synchrony in bodily ways of being—physiological, affective, and kinesthetic states—in particular sensorial environment.[13] Take, for example, how the national collectivity of Japanese people and their so-called blood ideology is produced through the exercise routine that is broadcasted on the radio and television everyday:

> Large numbers of people are doing the same movements at the same time across the country, and thus in kinaesthetic harmony with each other . . . [promoting] group loyalty and synchrony. . . . Blood in this case can be said to talk by moving multiple bodies in the same way at the same time. This is an example of community being sensed, not simply imagined.[14]

When individual bodies move in harmony with others, what one feels in one's body becomes what the larger society feels collectively. Social marginalization, stigmatization, or discrimination manifest to the extent that a body is not able, or allowed to belong to the experience of communal synchrony. Accessibility and accommodation for people with various degrees of abilities and disabilities mark the level of social inclusivity, widening the types of bodies that can belong, while simultaneously shifting the rhythm and movement of communal synchrony itself. In a broader sense, then, society is a sensory assemblage, a collectivity of feeling bodies that sense and feel with and for its members.[15]

In the following, we highlight the ways in which various sensory modes are engaged to sense and feel race. Using the conventional Western categorization of the five senses, we examine how each sensory mode—seeing, touching, tasting, smelling, and hearing—is technologized to produce particular assemblages of sensory embodiment and intensified bodily feelings about race. Such sensory embodiment and bodily feelings are at once private and collective, real and hegemonic, discursive and material, fleeting and tangible. We conclude the chapter by emphasizing the significance of bodily sensations and somatosensory experiences as a modality of racialization in which bodily senses function as a prosthetic technology that assembles and regulates various visceral sensations to make race a sensible, feel-able event.

Believing Is Seeing: The Racialized Vision

The idea that race is a visual construct does not require much convincing. Race is conventionally understood as the categorization of people based on their visible phenotypical characteristics, including the skin color, hair texture, body figure, and facial features. It is widely assumed that race is something we can see externally as evidence of one's race. The discursive, ideological, or social construction of race hinges, explicitly or implicitly, on the visibility of phenotypical differences marked on the body, making vision the primary mode of racialization. Such primacy of vision in racialized perception, however, is challenged by various scholars. For example, Jennifer Lynn Stoever repositions vision's dominance in racial theorizing by attending to the practice of listening as a mode of racialization.[16] She argues that the racial color line between whiteness and blackness is sonically drawn, cultivating the "listening ear" that actively discerns and discriminates various racialized sounds. According to Stoever, the visual construction of racial differences intertwines and is reinforced through the auditory mode of racial discernment by white subjects who listen to "black" music, singing voice, dialects, or accents.

Osagie K. Obasogie challenges the assumption that race is always visible and already self-evident on the surface of the body. He interviewed people who were born blind and found that a lack of vision does not prevent them from "seeing" the visual significance of race. Blind people are able to navigate racially coded social relations and learn to "see" race through social interactions and racial discourses just like sighted people.[17] His study illuminates the constitutive process through which race becomes visible and perceptible through social practices that give salience to racialized meanings of physical features. Nevertheless, blind people go through stages of uncertainty and make efforts to figure out the racial identity of people they interact with. Asia Friedman provides a slightly different account by arguing that blind people's race attribution is often uncertain and requires additional information seeking and interaction.[18] Friedman argues that the perceptual labor involved in blind people's experience of race demonstrates that "race is an interactional accomplishment," and "it is only through privileging vision over other modes of sensory perception that race can be experienced as 'self-evident.'"[19]

In his discussion on racial identification and vision, Martin Berger points out that visual images function as material evidence for our preexisting thoughts and beliefs. Berger states that "instead of selling us on racial systems we do not already own, the visual field powerfully *confirms* previously internalized beliefs."[20] The act of seeing race is a retroactive practice that materially verifies the tale of racial differences. In this case, what solidifies the mythical yet material truth of race is not the symbolic meaning assigned to the body (and our successful decoding of the meaning), but the cultivation of perceptual capacity to see bodily features as evidence of greater social and group differences. The act of seeing race is a powerful confirmatory practice that renders the visibility of race to seem natural while concealing its constitutive mechanism. The fact that we cannot *not* see race, then, is a historical accomplishment in which our ocular perception is cultivated to uphold and confirm the existence of racial differences as self-evident.

In a poignant anecdote on the primacy of seeing race, Solomon Gustavo, a black writer who grew up in Minnesota, describes an encounter with two white boys in his childhood:

> The first memory I have of feeling sad because I'm black came at age 6. Another kid was being pushed on a swing by his older brother. I saddled up next to them and nodded hello. The little boy looked at me and did a double-take. "Wait," he said, looking up at his brother, "so that's a nigger?" The older brother, perhaps all of 9, knew something very inappropriate had been said. He shuffled his younger brother away while the smaller boy kept asking, "What? Is that a nigger or not?"[21]

For this white body who saw a real black person for the first time in his life, his "first time" functions to confirm the existing stereotypes, stigma, and negative affect attached to blackness that he learned from others. What he saw is not a black person, but a black body as material evidence of what he heard and learned to feel about black people. Saturated by media images and social discourses about blackness, there is no genuinely pure act of seeing a black person *for the first time*. For the little white boy, seeing a real black person functions as a retroactive confirmation of stigmatized ideas about blackness that have been circulating interpersonally, socially, and historically. For this white boy, the perceptual primacy of seeing a real black body for the first time is paramount. A black person is no longer a fictive character seen on TV; the black body exists as a living body, a living proof of blackness. The black body that the white boy sees is entangled with meanings of how he has already learned to see blackness as the Other. What is even more interesting is the uneasy reaction of the older brother, who understood the offensive connotations of the word uttered by his younger brother, but did not quite negate his question. If "race is visually essentialized, or taken as something materially real and visually observable,"[22] is it possible for these white boys to see a black boy and not see a nig***?

The rhetoric of colorblind ideology presents an interesting ethical conundrum—"to see" or "not to see" race. Racial blindness is a double-edged sword. If one claims "not to see" race, one denies the existence of racism only to perpetuate the system of injustice. Statements like "I don't see color; I treat everyone as individuals" ring hollow in the face of ongoing systemic and institutionalized racism faced by people of color. But even trickier (and more revealing) is when one claims to "see" race in the spirit of anti-racism, because "seeing race" involves both social and physiological act of seeing in which social differentiation of races is built upon the visual perception cultivated through the history of racialization and racism. The double meaning of "seeing"—one as a social act and the other as an ocular perception—is at the core of the sensory metaphor of colorblindness.

The dilemma of the colorblind metaphor calls attention to the "sensory underpinnings of our culture"[23] in which our material bodies and senses are actively deployed to constitute, confirm, and reify socially constructed meanings. The ethical conundrum of colorblindness points to the role of the senses in constituting social reality, in which the social act of seeing race is "proven" through the physiological act of perceiving differences (i.e., colors, shapes, tones, and textures of differently racialized bodies). In this case, *seeing race* can be viewed as an attentional orientation cultivated through historical socialization of our senses, rendering what the eyes see as salient and meaningful characteristics of human bodies. Seeing race involves a cultivation of a body-subject that is oriented toward particular features of human bodies as socially and ideologically meaningful. Racial colorblindness remains a myth, not only because we cannot undo the ideological and institutional construction of race so easily but also because we cannot simply undo our embodied perceptual habit ingrained in our act of seeing racialized others.[24]

We cannot *not* see race because the social act of seeing race deploys our bodily senses that have been collectively and historically trained and cultivated to see, hear, and *confirm* race as a source of differences that matter.[25] Thus, when we claim that we cannot *not* see race in a move toward dismantling racism, it is important to attend to the sensory aspect of "seeing" race that is inherent in the reproduction of racial hierarchy as the institutionalized—and largely automated—system of social organization.[26] In the following section, we shift our focus to the tactile experience of pain as it relates to the historical construction of racial differences.

Touching the Other: The Racialized Pain

In connecting sensory experience with issues of power, Ruth Frankenberg writes, "Race privilege is the (non)experience of not being slapped in the face."[27] The comparison of privilege as a lack of painful sensation is not only intuitively revealing but also ideologically significant. If "to have pain is to have certainty, [then] to hear about pain is to have doubt."[28] It is through keeping the pain of racially disadvantaged others viscerally and experientially unimaginable or doubtful that reality of racism remains obscured and unarticulated. The pain of racism, historically and presently, is physically and viscerally felt by bodies of color. In this context, the non-experience of pain as a form of racial privilege, literally and metaphorically, becomes a powerful tool of racial oppression. The burden of proof is on the racialized Other whose pain is viscerally unimaginable to those who benefit from race privilege.

As one of the most prominent tactile sensations that are at once intimately personal, physical, and social, pain presents an interesting entry point into theorizing the role of the senses in constituting race and racial hegemony. Elaine Scarry postulates "the problem of pain is bound up with the problem of power," because pain is always beyond what words can describe and thus inexpressible in language.[29] Pain makes visible the complexity of physical experience that resists linguistic objectification. Such failure of language renders pain as one of the most tactical tools of political appropriation: "The failure to express pain . . . will always work to allow its appropriation and conflation with debased forms of power."[30] David Morris posits that the experience of pain is always historically and socially shaped, and asserts that the existential significance of pain is largely lacking in current medical discourses. Morris claims the encounter with pain "always contains at its heart the human encounter with meaning."[31] Despite the limitations of language, pain compels us to make meaning of this totalizing physical experience, and therefore pain is always more than impersonal and meaningless activities of nerves and neurotransmitters. Due to its visceral and perceptual nature, pain mediates the social and the sensorial. For example, linguistic expressions of abstract pain are often accompanied by sensations, visceral imaginations, or affective reactions of "as if" one feels real physical pain.[32] Abstract (social/cultural) pain and concrete (physiological/biological) pain cannot be so neatly separated in this case, pointing to the significance of the sensuous body in constituting social meaning.

Using the historical accounts of racist discourses and practices in the US South since slavery through the 1950s, Mark Smith provides disturbing examples of how the senses were used as a political tool of racism.[33] By examining "the role of the senses in structuring historical meaning,"[34] Smith illustrates how white southerners and slaveholders literally sensed—smelled, touched, heard, felt, and saw—blackness and black inferiority into existence. Southern whites developed what Smith called "sensory stereotypes" to censor racial passing that had become prevalent through the increased presence of biracial people. Whites believed in the "authenticating power of their senses" to differentiate blacks from whites in the increasingly mixed-race, visually ambiguous, environment by smelling, seeing, and touching blacks.[35] The construction of blackness—and the assumption of innate black inferiority—in the antebellum South was built upon the premise of the particularity of black senses and whites' ability to sense them out. Southern whites believed that "blacks as a group [naturally] smelled, that they sounded a particular way, [and] that their skin felt different."[36] Politicians, scientists, and anthropologists argued that blacks have less sensory capacities to appreciate aesthetic aspects of life, including art, music, and fine cuisine. Whites' cultural superiority was explained through blacks' inferior and underdeveloped sensory system to taste, listen, and enjoy the sophisticated culture of Western civilization.

Smith's account shows how race is not simply a social construction, but more fundamentally a sensory construction in which whites historically conditioned their visceral and emotional response to racial differences through sensory stereotypes. As Howes points out, "The transformation of class [or race] distinctions into physiological sensations is a powerful enforcer of social hierarchies."[37] Southern whites compared black slaves' sensibility to that of a child—infantile, simplistic, passionate, and indulgent. They argued that black slaves were suited for harsh physical labor because of their thick and supple skin, justifying forced and intense physical labor under the sun. More disturbingly, the white brutality and lynching against blacks were justified because whites believed that black skin is thick and numb—whereas white skin is thin and sensitive—to physical pain.[38]

What is most notable in the historical subjugation of African American people is not merely how black bodies were signified through racist sensory stereotypes; rather, it is the constitution of white subjectivity as dominant and normative sensory experience. In Smith's account, southern whites assumed authority not simply in social, political, and economic institutions but also in a more fundamental ability to exercise normative sensibility—the authenticating power of their senses to identify nonwhites; their sophisticated senses to appreciate high culture; and their sensory authority to determine how blacks feel pain on their skin. The dehumanization of black people was based on the denial of their personal and subjective sensory experience, in that white people assumed the authority to determine how much pain must be inflicted on black skin for blacks to feel it. Morris wrote that during slavery, the belief that "slaves were incapable of human feelings and desires" was used to justify racism, sustaining the "paradoxical article of faith among slaveholders that slaves did not feel pain."[39] In this context, whiteness can be viewed as an embodied sensory subjectivity that assumes itself as the normative, standard, *human* sensory experience.[40] The dichotomy between self and other in the process of racialization is formed through the construction of black "sensory otherness" against which the normative senses of whiteness are constituted.[41]

In her discussion on representations of whiteness in the black imagination, bell hooks problematized the authenticating power of white normative gaze: "In white supremacist society, white people can 'safely' imagine that they are invisible to black people. . . . As fantastic as it may seem, racist white people find it easy to imagine that black people cannot see them if within their desire they do not want to be seen by the dark Other."[42] To objectify others, one must take away their ability to sense the fullness of reality. The objectification of black people and other racial minorities is complete when their subjective sensory experiences are in doubt. In this case, whiteness becomes normative insofar as it is a form of hegemonic sensory order that renders racialized others' senses as not normal. Whiteness becomes an embodied location of sensorial authority that is entitled to claim how nonwhite others feel. This line of thought still shapes collective social imaginations of blackness today, in which hyper-sexualized, masculinized, or criminalized imaginations of black bodies are invoked to justify violence against them (and the pain inflicted on these bodies).[43]

Eating the Other: The Racialization of Taste

The mundane act of eating and tasting is deeply intimate, sensuous, and multisensory, as David E. Sutton claims taste is "an actual multisensory experience, which involves the dissolving of the object into the subject."[44] Closely interacting with the sense of smell, tasting food entails a range of visceral and qualitative sensations, such as color, flavor, texture, sound, and heat, that combine together to produce the multisensory experience of bodily sensations—delicious, comforting, nostalgic, energizing, fulfilling, refreshing, satisfying, disgusting, or bland. Eating food is essentially the most intimate form of touch, a touch between the subject (living body) and the object (food, which is also a form of lived beings). Cultural cuisines also trace transnational movements of people, spices, ingredients, and recipes, following the contours of colonial invasions, imperial power, global trade, and social stratification. Cultural dishes reveal "the relationship between taste as aesthetic practice and sensation . . . processes of collective bonding, inclusion and exclusion, cultural power, and people's agency therein."[45] At the same time, in the context of multiculturalism, "ethnic food has become the measure of one's tolerance of cultural diversity."[46] Interestingly, bell hooks used the expression of "eating the other" as a metaphor of cultural consumption by white subjects who seek pleasure, excitement, and transformation by commodifying and consuming the cultures of racialized Others.[47]

In his ethnographic study at a seafood trailer in East London, Alex Rhys-Taylor argues that the visceral sensations of disgust expressed toward the working-class seafood trailer actively mediate and construct social order and cultural categories of taste and distaste. Through his sensory ethnographic descriptions, Rhys-Taylor demonstrates that taste—not just cultural meaning of certain flavor, but the sensation of tasting itself—plays an active role in the formation of cultural identity and social order.[48] The "authenticity" or "tastiness" of a certain cultural dish is certified or confirmed on the tongue—it requires not only the dish prepared according to the "traditional" recipe and appropriate ingredients but also individuals whose taste has been cultivated according to the localized and habituated sensations of eating the particular dish. Such felt sensations of flavors and textures of food are deeply visceral and material, in that not only do we taste the food on the surface of our tongue but we dissolve it into our material body. The visceral sensation of food is a daily reminder of familiarity and foreignness, pleasure and disgust, and the known and unknown. The sensation itself is there to refer to and connote ideas and ideologies associated with certain flavors and people. What matters is a flavor triggers a physical and physiological sensation, onto which cultural meanings can be loaded. The sensation—of taste and distaste, pleasure, and disgust—itself becomes the material evidence of cultural codification of flavor and the people associated with it.

What is the role of taste in the formation of race and racial order? The visceral qualities of tasting food makes so-called ethnic cuisine an easy target of racialization—what tastes "exotic" or "different" functions as visceral evidence of sensory otherness and difference associated with a given racial group. In the book *Taste of the Nation: The New Deal Search for America's Food*, Camille Bégin examines the sensory economies of taste that functioned to demarcate racial, ethnic, and class lines in the 1930s and 1940s. As African Americans migrated north from the southern states, the taste of southern food evolved from "a taste of place to a sense of race."[49] Northern whites consumed southern dishes as "black food," which allowed them to gain "sensory satisfaction . . . grounded in the knowledge that one was crossing the line and indulging in a racial pleasure."[50] The racial line was reinforced by whites' sensory performance in which they demonstrated their ability to "recognize and navigate the racialized taste line" by consuming and commodifying food prepared by black people.[51] At the same time, the reconceptualization of black urban food as "soul food" enabled the unification of black identities across the southern and northern regions of the United States, working as a cultural site of resistance against racism. The regional classification of food simultaneously worked to draw racial lines, in which taste rhetorically produced and viscerally confirmed the imagined differences among racial groups.

Taste literally and physiologically invokes "gut feelings," merging the digestive and ideological dimensions of eating foods—what is not palatable on tongue is unlikely to be ideologically favored either. Take, for example, how "Asian food" is inseparable from the racialization of people of Asian descent. As one of the major categories of ethnic food in the United States, Asian food encompasses a wide range of cuisines originated in the vast geographical region in Asia that mutated into the local, "Americanized" foods through migration, transnational adaptation, and cultural appropriation. It is perhaps more accurate to say that "Asian cuisine" in the United States is really "Asian American cuisine." In the book *Dubious Gastronomy: The Cultural Politics of Eating Asian in the USA*, Robert Ji-Song Ku argues, "Asian Americans have always been and continue to be emblematic of the unassimilable American, not only in body politic but in gastronomic culture as well. Asian food is America's culinary stepchild, technically part of the family but never quite entirely."[52] In US popular culture, it is far more likely that a TV viewer comes across a scene where white characters are eating Chinese food from a to-go box with an awkward use of chopsticks than they see real Chinese American actors. It is far more likely to see a group of white characters at a Sushi restaurant than seeing Japanese American characters on the screen. Asian people are culturally sensorialized into the taste of their cuisine, while "Asian food" and "Asian flavor" seem to function as a sensorial evidence of the unitary "Asian race." As long as real Asian bodies remain relatively invisible in the public sphere, the tangibility of "Asian flavor" and its associated exoticness serve to reify Asians as unassimilable Americans. What could be more tangible than the taste, flavor, texture, and heat of food that touch our mouth and tongue? Even in the food metaphors of US multiculturalism—melting pot, salad bowl, and even chocolate fondue—Asian food is far removed from the imaginary of the "taste" of the nation. Ku posits, "Matters of gastronomy are a matter for a nation's sense of collective self as much as they are for its sense of collective taste. The ambivalence over eating Asian in the United States is reflective of a general tendency, and a considerable irony, in American immigrant history."[53]

For those who came from countries in Asia, "Asian food" in the United States is often removed from the tangible memories of flavor and taste of home. "Asian food" is a code word for the Americanized version of their ethnic or national cuisine, diluted for American consumers and restaurant goers, by way of making it less spicy, less raw, less exotic, and more localized, and culturally hybrid. It is not *authenticity* that is important here; rather, what is troubling is the *authentication* of Asian culinary and cultural otherness that is qualitatively experienced and viscerally confirmed when non-Asian restaurant goers dine at an "Asian" restaurant. Asian Americans remain unassimilable and forever foreign, partially but importantly because of the routinized sensory order in US culinary landscapes that reminds people, at the visceral level, of the foreignness of Asian culture and its taste.

Smelling Race: The Aroma under Our Noses

Chris once asked students, mostly white, in his intercultural communication course to talk about experiences where they came to know about their own racial identity. Unexpectedly, a white student answered by stating, "Every day I walk in my dorm hallway, there is always this smell. These people have the same odor, every day." Some students in the class quietly laughed, so Chris asked, "Who are these people and how do they smell?" Sensing that he was being challenged, the student sat in silence, but then stated, "I am not trying to be racist, but those Somali people have a strange smell. It is like a greasy, oily smell. I am not going to say it stinks. But, I believe we all have our own scent, right?" Chris replied, "So your white racial identity is understood through an odor that is familiar to you?" The student responded, "Yeah, I guess so. I mean, you asked us how we first came to know about our own race." Chris then asked, "Were you bothered by the scent of the residents?" The student replied, "Yes, I was. I am not going to say how it smelled but I was uncomfortable with it." Again, there was some light laughter from the other students in the classroom. The student continued, "Well, it's not them, it's their food or spices. You can smell it on them. It's not the kind of food that I would eat, so I don't have that kind of smell on me." Chris then asked, "Well okay, what is the aroma of white people? What is the essence of the smell on your body?" The student replied, "Well, I don't know, we don't have a smell." To which Chris responded, sarcastically, "I presume whiteness is not only invisible but is odorless as well. White people have a long-lasting freshness like the smell of a mint flavor gum, huh?" This anecdote demonstrates how people may construct racial differences through the sense of smell—when the white student perceives the smell of the Somali residents, he otherizes them in constructing his own sense of white identity by negating "the other as not-I" through differences in smell.[54]

Scholars examine the importance of smell in highlighting connections with identity, difference, memory, theorizing the self, and in managing social differences.[55] Of all the senses, smell is perhaps the least researched and oftentimes is superficially understood as one of the most mundane experiences in our daily lives.[56] Yet olfaction is a cultural experience; it is an epistemological lens of sensory knowledge through which we understand and conceive of social identities such as race, gender, and class. In their classical piece, Gale Peter Largey and David Rodney Watson point out that "odors, whether real or alleged, are often used as a basis for conferring a moral identity upon an individual or a group."[57] Marking a cultural group malodorous functions as a moral justification for avoiding, segregating, or discriminating against the stigmatized population. The seemingly intuitive sense of smell combines with the social engineering of gut reaction in response to the sight and smell of the Other.[58]

Smell is often a fleeting sense in that a scent or an odor may quickly dissipate after momentarily rankling our noses. In considering the above anecdote, however, the odor of the Somali residents is etched in the memory of the white student whose own racial subjectivity becomes even more solidified after classifying the unusual odor that surfaces under his nose. The perceptibly strange odor enabled him to sense racial otherness of Somali students, while normalizing his white racial subjectivity. Odor thus becomes a robust sensorial marker of racial and cultural difference, a status symbol or boundary marker actualizing his unscented white olfactory identity and (re)establishing his own distance from the racialized Other. The sense of smell demarcates the racial insiders and outsiders, where the white male student's olfactory assessments marginalize and denigrate these Somali residents as malodorous. As Classen asserts, members of the dominant group attribute the foul smelling stench to those in subordinated groups not as a response to their actual odor, but as a metaphor playing up their alleged decadence and depravity as a result of being the "Other."[59]

In his ethnographic study on the visceral politics of aroma and smell in Asian American communities in New York City, Marin F. Manalansan IV points out how the demarcation between the modern and the primitive is negotiated through olfaction.[60] The odorless-ness of the modern skyline is associated with logic and order, while the peculiar smell of ethnic communities and their food is associated with backwardness, uncleanliness, and chaos. The olfactory negotiations in public space—such as subway trains—become a site where supposedly odorless and privileged Manhattanites assert and justify racial segregation and spatial marginalization of communities of color. The possession over social/public space is expressed through the disapproval or even fetishization of "strange" odors of "exotic" food of immigrant communities. The immigrants themselves are aware of such olfactory stereotypes and try to contain and deodorize their food odors. The racialized construction of Asian American otherness and foreignness is not merely a visual and auditory demarcation (how Asians look or sound different), but also an olfactory struggle to keep out the strange aroma of newly arriving immigrants. The smell of otherness compels containment and discipline, while its porousness and transferability leave the threat of one becoming—and smelling—like the Other.

In his ethnographic analysis of "smellscape" in Singapore, Kelvin E. Y. Low demonstrates how racialized olfaction mediates the sense of place in racial enclaves.[61] The spatial demarcation of neighborhoods such as Little India, Little Thailand, and Little Myanmar is experienced through olfactory marking of these places as malodorous. The perceived malodor naturalizes racial stereotypes and class prejudices toward these communities, while justifying the segregation of migrants and foreigners in Singaporean society. As Low asserts, "Social bodies are not merely racial bodies; they are also, in effect, odourous bodies that signify [and mediate] race constructs."[62] To avoid the smell associated with those racial enclaves means to avoid both the place and the people who reside there. As an intimate form of contact, smell reminds us of the impossibility of total segregation in multicultural urban spaces. The olfactory stigma speaks to the intimacy of urban environment where the smell of otherness constantly threatens the sensory normativity and spatial segregation by the dominant group.

In her article exploring the gendered and racialized politics behind the use of vaginal deodorization, Michelle Ferranti argues that African American women are disproportionately impacted by olfactory discrimination and stigma.[63] Ferranti writes that while white women often voluntarily choose to use commercial products for vaginal deodorization, African American women report that social and cultural beliefs influence their decision to use these products. African American women are often introduced to douching by their mothers, and some even use homemade mixtures of vinegar and water, Pine-sol and water, or bleach and water for vaginal deodorization, despite the health risks of such methods. Ferranti concludes that racist beliefs about African American women's bodies and body odors, along with negative associations with sexual promiscuity, resulted in their regular use of vaginal deodorants. Such cultural stigma is historically rooted in slavery and segregation when whites established olfactory stereotypes about black people. African American women face culturally institutionalized norms and expectations to deodorize their body in the face of advertisers who exploit their insecurity about personal body odors.[64]

Olfactory meanings take hold of our bodies and are intertwined with the environment where our bodies gather information. Olfactory perceptions resonate with our own corporeal and somatic experiences including our connection to people and places. As seen in the story earlier, prejudice may emanate from aroma-fueled simulations, through odor in the food or on the body of an individual belonging to a particular ethnic group. Attributing foul, strange, or unusual odors to foreigners or racialized Others denigrates them, while white Americans are believed to harbor neither traces nor residues of scent. Attuning to olfactory politics reveals much about how the social designation of the Other is registered and confirmed at the visceral level, making it difficult to challenge such olfactory stigma. In the next section, we turn to sensory experiences of hearing to understand how auditory experiences mediate race, racialization, and racism.

Hearing Race: The Racialized Soundscape

Jennifer Lynn Stoever foregrounds the racialized practices of listening as fundamental to the construction of race and racialized subjectivity in the United States.[65] Using the notion of *the listening ear*, she calls attention to the socially cultivated mode of listening that amplifies white voice and renders the voices of color inaudible or insignificant, drawing what she calls *sonic color lines*. During slavery, white elites and slaveholders actively constructed the idea that black slaves sound and listen in certain ways by characterizing slaves' voices as "coarse" or "loud," and disciplining slaves' listening behaviors to perform obedience.[66] Black slaves were not only physically controlled but also aurally disciplined and terrorized. Such aural racism continued into the twentieth century, when the spread of radio broadcasting technologies further reinforced the racialized ways of listening. Stoever argues that whiteness and Americanness came to be merged through the racialized sonic citizenship that carefully demarcated the sounds of whites and nonwhites, establishing whites' listening practices as a universal and normative mode of listening. The racialized soundscape is constituted not only by the characterization of sounds as associated with certain races but also in terms of the modality of embodied listening that makes racial color lines audible.[67]

Ian Haney López uses the metaphor "dog whistle" to describe racial entreaties through which politicians use coded racial appeals in their campaigns to endorse policies that ultimately serve the rich and powerful, while undermining the interests of marginalized groups, including communities of color and working-class whites.[68] Haney López asserts that racial entreaties work very much like a dog whistle, a frequently inaudible sound that triggers strong reactions from those who are attuned to its race baiting tone: "Like a canine reacting to the piercing blast of a whistle, voters react to the subtext of political messages (e.g. welfare cheats, gangbangers, terrorists, or food stamp president), which hints to sharp, penetrating racial stereotypes of people of color."[69] Unlike the loud irritating sound of a normal whistle, humans hear a quiet hissing sound of the dog whistle that still, metaphorically, commands, controls, and trains them to think about race in particular ways. Haney López argues politicians blow the proverbial dog whistle by subtly hinting to racist stereotypes of people of color that incites racial animus in white voters. Politicians know that using blatant racist statements and appeals would be foolish, and therefore communicate in dog whistle terms to appear racially neutral.[70] Haney López's use of this sensorial metaphor associated with sound challenges the primacy of sight in conceptualizations of race and racism by examining sweeping coded racial appeals that are provoked by what we hear.

If whites aurally controlled and disciplined blacks, Stoever argues, African American writers, singers, and performers negotiated and challenged white normativity and racism by asserting themselves as listening and sounding subjects.[71] Resistance against racism entailed the aural politics in which African American subjects worked to make themselves sound and heard through literary works, singing performance, and musical creativity. Stoever provides an aural reading of W. E. B. Du Bois to point out the viability of black soundscape—lectures, music, spirituals, wails, shouts, and silences— that decries the visions of white supremacist representations of black life and culture.[72] The sound of black vernacular cultural expressions in the church, family gatherings, and hip-hop culture, and through Black English is, simply put, the sound of black people on the move. The tone and flow of rap, jazz, rhythm and blues music, and rhyme and rhythms of a poet or pastor, and the call and response of an audience all underscore the sound of *soul* in black experience, performance, and dialect.

Comparably, by asking "why does country music sound white?" Geoff Mann discusses how the values, traditions, and nationalism in the United States are tied to country music.[73] Mann claims that country music constructs an idealized, nostalgic past for whites whose identity and whiteness are (re) produced by what they hear. He argues the fact that white people perform, listen to, and purchase country music is a by-product of the sounds of whiteness and how it is heard. To be sure, Bill Malone stated, quite frankly, that the "singing voice of Charley Pride, the only non-white 'star' in the history of the [country music] industry, was so country that no one suspected he was black."[74] Mann thus concludes that trope of nostalgia in country music, in the context of an unapologetically American, Christian, and politically incorrect themes, produces a sound that hails white people to reimagine and reembody a past that reinvigorates an "authentic 'once was' in whiteness."[75] The nostalgic sound of country music thus performs the ideological work of forming and sustaining the materiality of race in the United States.

To the extent that our senses guide how we act within our experiences, racism conditions us to not only *see* and feel the world differently but also *hear* and feel it differently. The loud, fast, and thumping sound of hip-hop music or the slow, twangy, and string band sound of country music may indulge or assault the ears depending on one's lived, raced bodily existence. This is not to say that only black people are fulfilled by the rhythmic speech and scratching of the turntables in hip-hop music and that only white people revel in the blended sounds of banjos and Irish and Celtic tunes in country music. All ears hear music, but race compels us to consider how we might hear it differently. When a young white and black person, growing up in the inner city or suburbs in the late 1980s and early 1990s, hears the loud piercing, pulsating beats of the prelude to Public Enemy's song, "Fight the Power," or NWA's song, "Fu*k Da Police," before lyrics are expressed, they both may unreflectively and, at once, move their heads up and down heeding the rhythms and bass of the beat. But, a black person may immediately tune into the frustrations of police brutality—something that a white person may tune out as it is possibly not within the purview of their experiences. The sounds—cries, laments, and elations—reproduce race and racism, and *re-sound* racialized subjectivity and embodiment by way of, or on the far side of, other senses. The percussions and acoustic sounds of cultural expressions not only vibrate in the air and from the walls but also reverberate through, and within, the body that exists, feels, resists, and orients itself to *race*.

Conclusion

A racialized society emerges as a sensorial lifeworld that marks, regulates, and divides ways of sensing and feeling according to one's racial standing. Various sensory modes are deployed in marking, distinguishing, and reifying "us" versus "them." Race materializes through an intensification of certain visceral sensations and sensory perceptions—an assemblage of affective, bodily, and emotional habituations.[76] Race crystalizes into a social object by producing coordinated bodies that move, feel, and participate in the racial sensorium.[77] Race is a series of emergent and/or routinized sensorial events in which certain ways of feeling and sensing are intensified, unfolded, and made to stick to certain bodies and communities.

In his ethnography of trans culture and Western tourism in Goa, India, Arun Saldanha explains the notion of viscosity as follows: "Viscosity is about how an aggregate of bodies holds together, how relatively fast or slow they are, and how they collectively shape the aggregate (in this case, the aggregate of white youngsters in Shore Bar). Viscosity is also about how this holding together is related to the aggregate's capacities to affect, and be affected by, external bodies."[78] Saldanha uses the notion of viscosity more literally than metaphorically, referring to the open-ended and dynamic nature of human interaction and encounter. Race, according to Saldanha, is a "machinic assemblage" of bodies, movements, practices, sensations, places, and ideas, among many other elements.[79] Race is therefore "defined not simply by boundaries between self and other but by the lines of flight of its components."[80] On the one hand, visceral sensations and bodily feelings occur when bodies and their flows of movements "thicken" and hold together into racial formation. At the same time, visceral sensations and bodily feelings are themselves viscous—*felt bodily sensations make race and racialization stick and thicken.* From visible racial phenotypes, auditory dissonance in foreign accent or racialized music, imaginations of tactile sensations of others' pain, to exotic taste or unpleasant scent, various intermingled senses create viscous sensations that stick to our memories, habituated embodiment, and senses of normality and abnormality. Such viscosity of race is routinized, habituated, and institutionalized into relatively stable and recurring assemblages.

Analyzing race as a sensory assemblage allows us to elucidate the materiality of race not in terms of the "grid" of identity politics or an intersectional category, but in terms of how race coheres into an aggregate of sensory perceptions and sensuous feelings that amalgamate certain bodies, practices, and ideas. It also guides us to think carefully about the viscous nature of history and social structures, and what it takes to unstick the racist and oppressive assemblages. If race is feelingly assembled and becomes sticky, it seems evermore important to bring feelings back into critical analysis of race and racism. When race touches our senses to induce a felt sensation, such felt sensation works as a viscous matter to help the racial prosthetics stick to our embodied senses and sensorial lifeworld. The relationship between social subject (the feeling body) and social object (race) is coextensive; race requires the feeling body to stick to the social subject, while the feeling body extends its senses prosthetically through the social object (race). Race exerts its hegemonic presence when our bodies are extended into assemblages of racialized senses. To the extent race exists socially, dismantling race involves transforming the ways in which we inhabit and extend our bodies and senses toward one another.

As a social, historical, and sensory construction, race delimits our sensory openness into a structure of racist sensory apparatus, closing down the possibility of being, sensing, feeling, and relating otherwise. A phenomenological approach to the sensory dimensions of racial subjectivity reveals that racial reality is saturated with visual, tactile, auditory, olfactory, and gustatory qualities that appeal to our senses. We must politicize our seemingly mundane and normative bodily senses and perceptual habits surrounding race to take the problem of racism seriously today. Changing our conscious thoughts, discourses, and behaviors is not enough to end racism. We must attend to our perceptual habits and bodily ways of being that implicitly reinforce the process of racial stratification and discrimination. We must begin to collectively cultivate phenomenological mindfulness, bodily sensibilities, and intercorporeal imaginations to unstick and disengage racist sensory assemblages. As an emergent and shifting anchor of lived subjectivity, our bodies and senses remain open to that possibility.

3

The Face in the Racial Mirror

On Strange Feelings of Racialization

Do I look Asian to you? More specifically, *does my face look Asian to you? What do you see when you see my face?* It is likely these questions seem more pointless than thought provoking. If you take a quick look at my face, you will have your answer. I look Asian, plain, and simple. People may wonder if I am Korean, Chinese, or Japanese, but I look (East) Asian. It's interesting that I have to make no efforts to look Asian. I wake up every morning and try to look presentable; I drag myself to fit in my professional outfit, and slap some makeup on my face in an attempt to look awake, feminine, or attractive. While my physical appearance generally requires a certain degree of effort and intentionality, when it comes to my racial appearance, *I just am.* A glance is all it takes to render the defense of *race-is-a-social-construction* seemingly powerless (or pointless) to the fate of my racialization. What is even more revealing is to ask: *Do I look Asian to myself?* I look into the mirror and search for the racial truth of my embodiment. What makes me quintessentially Asian—is it my eyes, jawline, the shape of my nose, or the yellow undertone in my complexion? It is interesting how things that are supposedly socially constructed and malleable like race seem so viscerally concrete and material—within the racial regime of perception, race is literally built into my face. As Emily S. Lee postulates,

"In a profoundly intimate sense, one lives race through the immediacy of the particular differences of one's embodiment."[1]

Elsewhere, I described my experience of racialization as follows: "The experience of becoming the racialized Other—seeing my own body as evidence of my otherness—came with a strange sensation, as if my bodily substance had gradually morphed into some foreign material."[2] I felt this "strange sensation" both internally in my body and externally as a disruption in my relationship to the world, as if I was dislodged from the world in which I was previously grounded and securely oriented.[3] There was something deeply visceral and material about my experience of racialization. It was as if my body was called out to act, move, and feel differently in the newly discovered world of race. As I contemplate lived experiences of racialization, I return to the physical memory of the strange sensation I felt in my body as a source of insight into the multisensorial world of race and racism.

Growing up in Japan, I didn't consciously see my bodily appearance through a racial lens. From a historical perspective, the fact that I did not see myself as Asian was not a mere accident or some kind of localized colorblindness, but an outcome of careful ideological work in which Japan strategically distanced itself from the Asian race.[4] Since the late 1800s, Japanese politicians and intellectuals used ideologies of blood to distinguish Japanese people from the non-Japanese Other.[5] In some ways, my lack of racialization growing up in Japan was still a product of racial ideologies that carefully navigated and responded to the racializing gaze of the West directed toward the geopolitical region called Asia. To this day, Japanese people do not see or care to see themselves as racially Asian, drawing a clear line instead between the Japanese and foreigners (*gaikokujin*). After Japanese society and education carefully taught me to de-Asianize my national and gender identity, I moved to the United States and found myself being confronted with a racial mirror. What I see in the racial mirror, then, is not merely a mirror image of my physical (racial) feature, but a reflection of particular embodiment, a body endowed with a very different narrative, senses, and possibilities of being.

What does it mean to see myself in the mirror and see an Asian face? Before moving to the United States, as a teenager I would look at my face in the mirror and obsess about my imperfections, but what I saw was nonetheless my own face. Perhaps I saw a Japanese woman, but not an Asian woman in that my self-perception was not racialized. Over the course of two decades in the United States, my daily routine of looking at myself in the mirror has slowly and gradually morphed into the act of looking at an Asian woman. Unlike the abrupt and totalizing experience of being called out—"Look, a Negro!"—described by Frantz Fanon,[6] my racial interpellation was subtle, slowly alienating myself from my own face. My face was no longer entirely mine; it was something others saw and they saw an Asian face. How is it possible that the face so familiar to me—my own face—appears perpetually foreign, exotic, and "oriental" to others? Someone asked me if I was an Asian actress they saw on TV; someone called me by the name of another Asian colleague; and people from other Asian countries/ethnicities would walk up to me and ask if I'm from their country or ethnicity. One time, a white male student enthusiastically greeted me in the hallway thinking I was his finance professor. On his face, I saw myself being recognized as his favorite professor, although I had never met this student. In the slightly awkward encounter, I gathered he mistook me for another faculty member in a different department. Many weeks later, I went to a workshop and saw the particular individual whom (I assume) the student mistook me for—a female faculty member from China. I knew of her, but we didn't know each other. It was a strange feeling; I was looking at a visual reminder of what I look like (to the white male student). Imagine the feeling: running into your double who looks nothing like you and exactly like you at the same time. Imagine the feeling: looking into the racial mirror and realizing what looks like you simultaneously appears foreign and familiar to your own eyes.

A woman who appeared white once lamented to me that people think she is white, but her grandmother is of Native American descent, implying that she is not really white, and proclaiming "it's not just about color." I found her need to assert her non-whiteness very interesting, because the reverse is not possible for me. As a woman who appears Asian, it seems utterly pointless to proclaim to the world that I'm not *really* Asian, even though the unity of "Asian" as a racial, cultural, or political category is a myth. If anything, such ethnic unity is a product of, and response to, racialization and racism. In her discussion on the question of authenticity of women of color, Lee wrote, "Endemic to the embodiment of women of color are perceptions that they always represent their culture and others resembling their bodies."[7] What's most significant in this transnational metamorphosis of my own body is not that the social meaning of my body has changed, but the fact I myself can no longer shed the perception of my own otherness, as "racialized bodies are not only seen as naturally inferior, they *cannot be seen otherwise.*"[8]

Racialization is a "codified perceptual act"—a process through which certain ways of sensing are activated and confirmed as truth.[9] My body is inscribed with racial meanings and stereotypes about Asian people that are historically constructed and reproduced. What I find significant to explore, however, is not what such inscription means symbolically (or how "constructed" it is); rather, I'm interested in exploring how such racial inscription feels on my body. I am curious about the nature and origin of the "strange sensation" I felt in becoming a racialized subject. The strange sensation I felt reminds me of the fact that my body is not simply an object of social inscription; my body actively feels the world, including the strange sensation of racial inscription itself. Even if racialization objectifies the surface of my visible face, my face is still here, feeling the force, weight, and texture of the racialized world.

This chapter provides a somatic self-reflection on the phenomenology of racialization by seeking insight into the "strange sensation" of racialization and its multisensorial dimensions. In reflecting on the felt-bodily experiences of becoming Asian, I begin by examining the face as a multisensorial location of intersubjective encounter. Alongside and underneath the mask of racialization, the face is an open field of intersubjective encounter whose shape, texture, and movement are contoured through interpersonal exchange and lived experience. The face invites, compels, yearns, and obligates us to feel with and for others. I focus on the role of the racializing gaze and stereotypes in immobilizing one's face, rendering it as a static object. I argue that racism targets the face, not merely because of its visual significance and visibility, but because the face is otherwise a dynamic and kinesthetic location of encounter with others. To uphold and maintain a racist society, the face must be destroyed and drained of its energy for intersubjective connection. The kinesthetic dimensions of face-to-face interaction lead me to consider the role of haptic visuality[10] in racialization. I address how the racializing gaze is experienced as a tactile sensation by racialized subjects, and therefore racism and racialization surface *sensationally* on one's skin. The chapter concludes by considering racialization in terms of affordance in space, or how we move through the world and how the world affords our movement. Taken together, the chapter illuminates how racialization engages and deploys multiple and intertwined assemblages of the senses.

The Face as a Multisensorial Location of Intersubjective Encounter

It is a mistake to approach the human face as simply a convenient signifier of racial category and stereotype. As a mirror into one's sense of self and a medium of intersubjectivity, the face exemplifies the nature of the human body not merely as an object of signification but also as a very subject of communication. That is, the face is not only a primary visual identifier of an individual but also a "material organ of communication."[11] The face is not simply a surface on which our cognitive and emotional states are exhibited; rather, ideas and emotions materialize, and are made sensible, through the dynamic and nuanced movements of the face. The face is a site of dynamic embodiment of self in relation to, and in the presence of, others. Imagine you find something really funny but are not allowed to smile or laugh. Would you be able to experience the amusement to its fullest extent if you couldn't express it physically on your face? The face is not a passive receptor of our thoughts and emotions, but rather it actively performs and materializes our thoughts and emotions. When something really funny happens, isn't it the felt sensations within your body—the vibration of your body through the laughter, the hands being clapped, the facial muscles lifted, and the mouth wide open— that make you feel good? Isn't the quality of felt sensations of bodily response a part of something being "funny"? And isn't it the sharing of these bodily sensations with others that makes the experience even more pleasurable? In face-to-face interactions, individuals engage in a flow of mutual exchanges of facial expressions and gestures. Our conversations are guided, punctuated, and made alive through rhythmic attunement with others' facial movement and expression. The face is "the embodied foundation of social relations."[12] The face, thus, is a part of the complex bodily apparatus of communication.

One of the very first ways the face starts to serve its social function is when an infant imitates their caretaker's facial gesture. This starts as early as the infant's birth. As infants perceive their caretaker's facial gesture (i.e., tongue protrusion), they experiment with their own mouth and tongue to imitate it. Experiments have shown that infants can engage in what they call "invisible imitation" in which imitation is performed by a body part that cannot be seen by the one who is imitating, such as their face.[13] At a very early stage in life, babies learn how to use their facial muscle by imitating other's facial expression. Research in child psychology and neuroscience shows that this imitative function ingrained in the face is key to developing a sense of self, relational connection, and intersubjectivity such as empathy.[14] That is, facial imitation—and attunement—is a way into feeling how others feel through embodiment of other's facial expression, as "the face . . . may have evolved not simply to display complex affective inner states but for those to influence the observer to feel the same."[15] Facial imitation is not simply about manipulating the face to look like someone else's face, but to tune into the affective and emotional state of the person who is being imitated. In this case, kinesthetic attunement through moving one's face is as important (if not more) as visual recognition of emotion expressed on one's face.

The face is a location of intersubjective encounter, as "the face is that essential fragment of the body that makes the social bond possible through the responsibility and recognition with which it endows the individual in his or her relationship to the world."[16] My face is the location where I receive and absorb others' faces. When I look at my three-year-old son's big smile (the kind of smile that overtakes his whole face, a genuine expression of joy and happiness), in that moment I forget about what my face is doing; or rather, my face becomes his, as my face melts and morphs into his smile. I absorb the sheer pleasure of facing his face, looking at him smiling at me, absorbing his cheerful nature, as Merleau-Ponty writes, "I live in the facial expression of the other, as I feel him living in mine."[17]

My face is many things in many situations. It is with my own face that I face the world. My face orients my whole body, directs my attention, and guides others' attention to (or away from) me. My face and its directionality inform my intentionality, commitment, and relationship with others. When I *face* challenges in life, such expression is not simply metaphorical, but a corporeal gesture of confronting the issues face-to-face. In his discussion on phenomenology of boxing, Jon D. Rutter points out the centrality of the face as a site of all experiences: "Many of our most powerful human expressions come from facial behavior, facial movements, facial gestures: we speak, we wink, we stare, we kiss, we cry. . . . As a site of both perceptual reception and existential expression, the face is a complicated place."[18] My face spreads with joy, shrinks with sadness, freezes in fear, opens with epiphany, and rests in calmness. I feel the active movement of my face both internally within my skin and externally as a dynamic visual expression and culturally coded facial gesture.

The face is also a material and expressive trace of selfhood. The face makes visible various traces of genetic, genealogical, familial, racial, and personal history. In her autobiographical writing, Ruth Ozeki chronicles her three-hour-long experiment in which she stared at her face in the mirror for three consecutive hours. As a biracial woman with a Japanese mother and a white father, she reaches the following conclusion after three hours of observing every detail on her face:

> My face is and isn't me. It's a nice face. It has lots of people in it. My parents,
> my grandparents, and their grandparents, all the way back through time
> and countless generations to my earliest ancestors—all those iterations here
> in my face, along with all the people who've ever looked at me. And the light
> and shadows are here, too, the joys, anxieties, griefs, vanities, and laughter.
> The sun, the rain, the wind, the broom poles, and the iron fences that have
> distressed my face with lines and scars and creases—all here. . . . Say hi to
> your face, face. Say hi to the world.[19]

Ozeki points out how her face is an accumulation of all people related to her, biologically or otherwise, and all her experiences that physically and spiritually marked and molded her face. Claiming that "a face is a time battery, too, a stockpile of experience,"[20] Ozeki speaks to the idea that all her memories, experiences, and relationships are impressed upon her face genetically, socially, culturally, and kinesthetically. She shows how the face does not exist as an independent object in the world, but as a sensuous interface between her and the world—the face is molded into its dynamic shape, texture, and action as it touches and is touched by the world. Another biracial writer, Chris Abani, similarly reflects on all the traces left on his face that are both physically marked and sensorially felt. He describes his face as follows:

> A face worn in by living, won in by suffering, by pain, by loss, but also by
> laughter and joy and the gifts of love and friendship, of family, of travel,
> of generations of DNA blending to make a true mix of human. I think of
> all the stress and relief of razors scraping hair from my face. Of extreme
> weather. Of rain. Of sun. I think of all the people who have touched my
> face, slapped it, punched it, kissed it, washed it, shaved it. All of that human

contact must leave some trace, some of the need and anger that motivated that touch. This face is softened by it all. Made supple by all the wonder it has beheld, all the kindness, all the generosity of life.[21]

Abani uses various tactile references about the contact between his face and the world—scratchiness of shaving his face with razors, changes in weather and temperature, physical touch of affection and pain caused by others, and the very presence of other human beings who touched his face both literally and metaphorically. For both Ozeki and Abani, the ontological significance of the face is that the face is a repository of sensuous memories.

Through countless face-to-face encounters and facial experiences, my face has become the "I" that faces the world. I'm not trying to reduce my selfhood to my face; rather, I'm trying to point out how numerous exchanges of facial gestures and experiences of (non)recognition have left traces and marks on my face, softening my face with the grace of smile and embrace, and hardening it with moments of hardships, rejection, and pain. What my face looks like is an ongoing outcome of such profound encounters and experiences, each of which leaves traces on my skin and memories in my facial muscle. The face is an embodiment of self not merely because of its visual and representational quality, but because the materiality of one's face is shaped by their embodied experiences. As one goes through life experiences, the face shows the signs and traces of joy, happiness, suffering, or trauma on its surface and movements. That is, the face goes through various metamorphoses in shape, texture, and movement that are not only determined by innate structure or visible composition, but also by personal life experiences. That is, the face is actively contoured by the forces of life. The face is not something that is already there as a visible object; rather, the face appears as an outcome of social, bodily, and intersubjective interactions. The significance of the face lies not only in its visual presence but also its kinesthetic movement that enables us to experience emotion, thought, affect, interpersonal relationships, and self-understanding with others.

Your Face Is a Mirror of My Face: The Gaze, Face, and Intersubjectivity

While various things shape the material appearance of the face—from the genetic makeup, scars from childhood injury, to overall life experience—the face, more than any other body part, seems to present itself to be looked at by others. The face invites, or even compels, us to look at it. The face—and the eyes in particular—has a gravitational force to open mutual self-other relations unlike any other body part.[22] Beata Stawarska argues that one comes to know the contours of his or her face not merely by visually perceiving their face (such as a reflection in the mirror) but also through the process of being seen by others and kinesthetically and proprioceptively responding to such gaze.[23] Our visual perception of our own face is always mediated by things such as a mirror image, photograph, or painting. In fact, we come to know very little about our faces by looking into the image of a static face in the mirror. Instead, we come to know our faces by looking at others look at our faces, observing the nuanced movements of their facial expressions, and experiencing our own faces move and be moved in response to others' facial gestures. Phenomenologically speaking, the face is a place where the "I" comes to appear—and disappear—within the intersubjective exchange of gaze and recognition.[24] The act of looking or being looked at is a dynamic kinesthetic process—we do not capture a static image of a face in face-to-face interactions; we move and are moved as we look at one another's face. The act of looking at the face takes place not merely as visual perception, but as embodied, rhythmic, and reciprocal movements of interpersonal exchange.

One's visual and proprioceptive knowing of their own face is constituted within face-to-face interactions with others' faces. The face is one of few body parts one cannot directly perceive; it is mediated by a mirror image or photograph. The other's face functions as a mirror that reflects one's face, as "being seen by others during face-to-face interaction provides an indirect experience of one's visible facial exterior."[25] Following Sartre's discussion on gaze, Florentina C. Andreescu claims, "Self-identity (and sense of security) is constructed not only by one looking at oneself, but also by one looking at others looking at one and one's attempt to reconstitute and alter these views of others."[26] My face comes to appear in the faces of others who look at my face, not only visually but in the combination of various felt experiences on my face. In this sense, the significance of the face is not simply about its visual quality but the proprioceptive, tactile, and kinesthetic materiality of one's face that emerges through interactions with others. The gaze mediates the visual perception of another's face and motor function in the act of facial imitation. In being seen, we come to "see" and feel our own face. In seeing another's face move, we move our face and proprioceptively understand the contours of our faces. Our facial embodiment is literally what connects us with others materially and experientially. The dynamic and kinesthetic nature of our face allows us to experience others and their embodiment almost synchronously, and in those rhythmic exchanges, intersubjectivity and empathy become possible. Through interpersonal exchange, the gaze sets into motion a dynamic loop of facial expression, visual perception, kinesthetic action, and proprioceptive feeling that constitute an embodied subject.

A Static Face in the Racial Mirror: Why Racism Targets the Face

What happens when the gaze that contours the face is a racializing one? Racialization is an act of objectifying and codifying one's facial and bodily features. Racialization is a process in which the face is coded into a sign, through which the face becomes "readable" in a fixed system of signs. While race is always more than visual appearance, how we make sense of someone's race largely depends on what his or her face looks like (including the color of skin on the face). When it comes to race and racialization, what is seemingly the signature of one's individuality is reduced into certain features that represent their race. The history of racial science shows how the facial structure and features have been measured and characterized as the evidence of inherent racial differences, including the shape of eyes, nose, cheekbones, lips, skulls, and jawlines. In everyday social interactions today, the question about one's racial identity still relies heavily on what is seen on the face. While the myth of scientific racism has long been debunked, in everyday encounters one's race is believed to correspond to racial features visible on the face. In many cases, a person's race is presumed self-evident on his or her face; when it is not self-evident (i.e., mixed race individuals), it invites curiosity and questions from others.

Despite the fact that racial differences are first recognized on one's face, not much attention has been paid to the significance of the face in terms of racial embodiment. Although the social meaning given to certain racial features may be critiqued, the assumption that we see race on the face is largely unquestioned. That is, we may critique the illogic and immorality of seeing civility on a white face and barbarity on a black face, while leaving the nature of the relationship between race and the face unexamined. Not only is the face racialized, race is facialized—our racial differences are reduced and reified into certain features that are believed to be universally shared among a group of people, not scientifically, but commonsensically. In some ways, to be racialized means to be facialized, the process of being reduced into a particular version of one's face in particular visual schema and context. The racializing gaze sets into motion a particular constitutive mechanism of subject-object relations.

Much discussion has been generated on the notion of gaze in the context of identity politics and the formation of subjectivity. In feminist scholarship, the gaze is discussed to illuminate the gendered relations of power in which feminine subjects become the object of the masculine gaze in patriarchal society.[27] The pressure for women to smile in public is a material example of how the masculine gaze contours the feminine face, urging women to literally move their facial muscle to conform to the gendered expectation to appear pleasant, happy, and approachable. Conversely, when male pedestrians refuse to cross the street when female drivers yield at the pedestrian crossing, it appears they are trying to preserve their masculine control by refusing their bodies to be moved by (feminine) others. Instead of hurrying their way as the drivers patiently watch and wait, those male pedestrians gesture to female drivers to keep driving and then take their time crossing the street afterward. They seem uncomfortable to be looked at, much less be moved or ushered by feminine subjects. In the context of racial politics, the so-called ethnic plastic surgery in which individuals surgically modify their "ethnic" facial features to those of another race (typically to model white racial features) is an example of the material contouring of the face infused with racial ideologies. The gaze is not an abstract concept, but an embodiment of power relations that materially shape how the bodies occupy and extend into social space.[28] In the context of unequal social relations of power such as race and gender, the gaze is not a neutral exchange of shared social bond. Rather, the subject-object relation constituted in the act of looking is a historical accomplishment in which the looker exercises power over those who are looked at.

To be the object of a racializing gaze means to be racially identified by one's face in which their face is viewed as a sign of racial category, measured by "degrees of deviance to the White man's face."[29] To be racialized, in this sense, is to be reduced into a static and monolithic image of the racially generalized facial features. It makes one's face a static object. This experience is deeply problematic if, as discussed earlier, we come to "see" our face based on the image reflected on others' face. Searching for an image of oneself in the gaze and face of others, one cannot find a dynamic face, but instead a static surface that does not move or change. The racialized face finds itself trapped in the stereotypical images that circulate in the media—either Asians in the United States don't see Asian bodies represented at all, or the representation is limited to the nerd, the overachiever, the martial artist, the seductive mistress or submissive housewife, the patriarchal misogynist or emasculated comic relief, the perpetual foreigner with strong accent or the yellow peril. Racial stereotypes function as a mirror on which the racialized subject comes to see their face reflected. Racial stereotypes are problematic not only because of generalization and denigration of racial groups but more importantly because of their phenomenological impact on those who are stereotyped. When the phenomenological gravity of the face is considered, racial stereotypes do not simply arrest one's face visually, but it also fixes their dynamic face into a condition of immobility.

To see my face as an object is not purely a visual experience, but I experience it as a kinesthetic one. I feel like I cannot move my face, or change the image of my face reflected in someone else's gaze. That is, I myself freeze in the image of my own racialization. What traps me is not the racialized image of my face, but the proprioceptive sense of inability to move (the image of) my face. Race is embodied not simply as visible physical features, but as a feeling of numbness and lack of motility on one's face as the object of the racializing gaze. David H. Kim points out three predominant forms of anti-Asian stigma, including "the aesthetic devaluation of Asian faces and bodies," "the derogation of alleged Asian personality traits . . . in terms of passivity, nonindividuality, or social ineptness," and "the derogation of alleged Asian foreignness, alienness, or being a FOB (Fresh Off the Boat)."[30] Kim elaborates on the feelings of racial shame and self-contempt in response to these forms of stigma. When the feeling of my racialization is heightened, my face is no longer a dynamic field of intersubjective encounter. The racializing gaze freezes my face and disrupts the face-to-face attunement and rhythmic exchange of facial gestures with others.

In her discussion on racializing gaze, Helen Ngo elaborates on the gaze in terms of "the quality of seeing" and points out how the racializing gaze entails "a *non-seeing*."[31] To be racialized means to be looked at, but never seen. This explains the paradox of racial hyper-visibility in which racialized subjects experience the scrutinizing and objectifying gaze but feel invisible or nonexistent. Such racial invisibility can also be understood as immovability or hindered motility—a disruption in the dynamic exchange and rhythmic attunement of emotional and affective states in face-to-face communication with others. To experience the racialization of one's face is not merely symbolically problematic; it is kinesthetically hindering, alienating oneself from one's own face. Racism targets the face, not merely because of the face's symbolic significance and visibility, but because the face is otherwise a dynamic and kinesthetic location of encounter with others, a field of possibility that allows us to materially feel the emotional and affective states of other living beings. As a dynamic location of intersubjective encounter, the face opens up communication and compels us to feel with and for others. To uphold and maintain a racist society, the face must be destroyed and drained of its energy for intersubjective connection. Le Breton argues that the "enigma of the face" is destroyed and vilified to justify racism: "Racism is never pure opinion, but anticipation of the murder that already begins through the symbolic liquidation of the other's face. If he no longer has a human shape, killing him is a public hygiene measure."[32] The face then becomes a key instrument of racialization and racist oppression, not merely as a visual reminder of supposed racial differences, but as a wall that blocks the very possibility of intersubjective connection and intercorporeal empathy.

Haptic Visuality and the Racializing Gaze

In face-to-face interactions, our faces move in response to, and in attunement with, the facial gestures and expressions on others' faces. The racializing gaze immobilizes the face from a dynamic organ of self-expression and intersubjective connection to a static image of racial stereotypes. There is a kinesthetic dimension to the experience of receiving a racializing gaze, and such experience is not strictly a visual one, but a disruption of the face-in-motion that is fundamental to developing intersubjective relations with others. In other words, the racializing gaze *touches* the racialized subject in ways that are more than the inscription of symbolic meaning on the surface of the body.

In this section, I elaborate further on the tactile experience of racial otherness by examining the interconnection between the racialized act of seeing and touching. How does the racializing gaze touch the racialized Other? How is the touch of the racializing gaze felt on the skin of the racialized subject?

In her analysis of intercultural cinema, Laura U. Marks uses the term "haptic visuality" to refer to tactile dimensions of visual experience, in which "the eyes themselves function like the organs of touch."[33] In contrast to optical visuality in which the viewer maintains a safe distance between the viewer and the object, haptic visuality arouses in the viewer a multisensory engagement with material texture, sensuous qualities, and affective charge of the object being viewed. Marks demonstrates how visual images provoke the viewer's multisensorial body memory rooted in their cultural belonging and diasporic experience. The act of viewing is never completely visual; vision intersects with and is substantiated by other sensory perceptions and memories, such as touch, smell, and taste. According to Marks, the experience of cinematic spectatorship is multisensorial, and the meaning of visual image is shaped not merely by the material content of the image but also by the related bodily feelings invoked by the image.[34]

Following Marks's insight into the multisensoriality of visual experience, it is useful to think about the haptic dimensions of the racialized vision. The racialized vision accompanies various multisensorial feelings, whether or not such feelings are registered consciously by the individual. The act of seeing race is substantiated by those implicit feelings that register as nonvisual information. The codified perceptual act of seeing race is always more than a simple exercise of connecting a certain signifier (darker skin) with a proper signified (exotic); rather, seeing bodies of color as exotic is accomplished and substantiated by nonnormative qualities, textures, and sensations associated with, or invoked by, the presence of nonwhite bodies. The explicit symbolic meaning attached to the body is less significant than the pre-reflective feelings and sensuousness invoked by what one sees on the body. To be more precise, the "gut feeling" that drives racial stereotyping is far more powerful and problematic than superficial labels and categorizations.[35] Therefore, critical analysis of visual representation of race may yield greater wisdom and insight if the analysis entails not only what appears in the image visually but how the visual image appeals to the viewer's tactile, kinesthetic, olfactory, or gustatory feelings in the body. The notion of haptic visuality challenges us to reflect, somatically and phenomenologically, on the multisensorial nature of seeing race. Haptic visuality is active and crucial in the perceptual construction and experience of race.

Expressions such as "piercing gaze" and "cold stare" indicate how the experience of being looked at is somatically registered as, or entangled with, skin sensations. There is a tactile quality to the experience of receiving a racializing gaze. The bodies of color receive such racializing gaze not merely as visual information but also as a tactile experience in that the gaze is felt on the skin. Le Breton points out that a sensory experience of viewing grants the looker a type of tactile or haptic sensation: "Touching not with the hand but instead with the eye, it seeks to make contact, to perform a kind of caressing motion. While the optical eye maintains a distance . . . the haptic eye inhabits its object."[36] Conversely, the racialized subjects inhabit the haptic sensation of being viewed as an object, as Frantz Fanon speaks to the "epidermal schema" of racialization.[37] While racism objectifies the body—and the skin—by sealing its surface with various signifiers, in the past two decades of my life in the United States, my skin never stopped feeling. In the dominant imagination of the racialized Other, it seems almost unimaginable (or un-feel-able) that racialized subjects still feel the world as subjects of their own experience. Racism makes the perceptual and sensorial experience of racialized subjects unimaginable, treating them as senseless objects. As a sensorial receptor and largest organ in the human body, however, the skin is not passively awaiting the inscription of racist meaning. Rather, the skin actively feels the impressions made on its surface, such as the sensations of racialized treatment and tensions in racially charged spaces. Sara Ahmed describes the experience of racism as sensations on the skin: "To feel negated is to feel pressure upon your bodily surface; your body feels the pressure point, as a restriction in what it can do."[38] Racism penetrates our skin, not because the skin color is racialized, but more fundamentally because our skin is sensitive and responsive to the touch of racism impressed upon our skin.

From the Visual Economy of Race to the Racialized Politics of Affordance

If race entails the politics of the skin, racialization generates a particular relationship between the racialized subject and their skin, in which they are constantly reminded of its appearance, meaning, and potential consequences. The skin is where self and the world meet, not as an impenetrable wall, but as an organ that materializes the feeling of being-in-the-world. The pulse of the world and others is felt on our skin.[39] Marc Lafrance reminds us that "forgetting about the skin is, in many respects, a privilege—one from which those with racialized skin are less likely to benefit."[40] The racialized sensorium creates a particular kind of "skinscape," not necessarily the one based on the "intimate association between the surface of the body and the surface of the earth, or landscape"[41] but rather one that disrupts such contiguity and integrity.

To ask what kind of world is "touchable" and felt on one's skin is always a political question.[42] Think, for example, about the tactile quality associated with femininity and masculinity. It is not just that the feminine skin is desired to be soft and smooth (and free of unwanted hair); a feminine subject is encouraged to touch and embrace the world gently. It is not just that the masculine skin is deemed coarse; a masculine subject is encouraged to interact with the world with hardness and roughness when giving a strong handshake, playing physical sports, or enduring pain. Touch is fundamental in everyday relations of power in that power is exerted by demarcating the line between those who touch as subjects and those who are touched as objects. Socially constructed differences are not merely marked on our external appearances; they are also felt on our skin and such felt sensations are *meaningful* in constituting the sense of self. Subjectivity emerges or concretizes when one feels something (encounter with the world) and feels oneself feel (encounter with the self).

Rather than examining race as a purely visual economy, a multisensorial approach allows us to take into account how social experience materializes on and through the feeling body. Racialization, in this case, is more than a visual signification of the surface of the body, but the politics of touch and skinscape—how the world touches us, and how we are habituated to reach toward the world.[43] Racism fundamentally disrupts and distorts the integrated sense of touching and being touched by the world. Living in a racialized body is like trying to live in a perpetual disintegration of mind, body, and environment. If *emplacement* describes the "sensuous interrelationship of mind-body-environment,"[44] racialization displaces and disharmonizes such unity. What people see on your face is not the same as what you think you are presenting on your face. It is as if you are smiling but all they see is a blank face. After so many repeated interactions, you begin to think your smiley face is indeed a blank face. What is left is a residue of contradiction between your muscle memory and its racially coded interpretation.

If racialization and racism constrict one's embodiment, the experience of (racial) privilege can be understood as a tactile and kinesthetic experience of emplacement, in which the social and material environment affords and extends their body. Ahmed describes the phenomenology of whiteness in terms of its felt expansiveness in one's spatiality, and therefore:

> To be not white is to be not extended by the spaces you inhabit. This is an uncomfortable feeling. Comfort is a feeling that tends not to be consciously felt. . . . You sink. When you don't sink, when you fidget and move around, then what is in the background becomes in front of you, as a world that is gathered in a specific way.[45]

The idea of "home" invokes various felt textures and sensorial qualities; a home is imagined to be warm, gentle, welcoming, accepting, and comfortable. In her discussion on the experience of migration and identity, Ahmed describes "the lived experience of being at home . . . [as] inhabiting a second skin," claiming that the sense of being at home emerges when "the subject and space leak into each other, inhabit each other."[46] Rejecting the idea that home is a fixed physical location to leave from or return to, Ahmed claims, "Being at home is here a matter of *how one feels or how one might fail to feel*."[47] In other words, being at home entails a feeling of sinking into spaces where the boundary between the self and world is blurred, or the self and the world are coextensive. It is the feeling of being embraced by and immersed in the environment, whether it is a physical space, people, natural landscape, temporal rhythm, or even simply the air we breathe.

The feeling of "being at home" is most immediately registered on one's skin, as a felt resonance and synchronicity between one's body and its environment. The opposite of being at home, then, is the feeling of displacement and out-of-place-ness felt on the skin. Ahmed provides an astute observation of whiteness as spatio-tactile experience: "Whiteness may function as a form of public comfort *by allowing bodies to extend into spaces that have already taken their shape. Those spaces are lived as comfortable as they allow bodies to fit in; the surfaces of social space are already impressed upon by the shape of such bodies.*"[48] Responding to Ahmed, George Yancy describes the experience of whiteness as follows: "To be white in a white world . . . is to be extended by that world's contours. The world opens up, reveals itself as a place called home, a place of privileges and immunities, a space for achievement, success, freedom of movement."[49] By contrast, "To be black in 'the white world' is to turn back towards itself, to become an object, which means not only not being extended by the contours of the world, but being diminished as an effect of the bodily extensions of others."[50] Racialization materializes as the body extends into or is diminished by the sociocultural space that embraces or marginalizes various bodies differently. Whiteness, then, may be conceptualized as a particular form of bodily movement, of moving bodies, and how the bodies are allowed, cultivated, and afforded to move in space. Racialization, therefore, is not merely a visual signification of the phenotypical surface of racial groups, but a construction of intersensorial space in which certain bodies inhabit as "homely," while others do not. Thus, racialization materializes in the very possibility of movement of the body, not just what the body looks like.

Conclusion: On Strange Feelings

A somatic self-reflection on the strange sensation of racialization illuminates the intersensorial dynamics of face-to-face interactions, gaze, haptics of vision, and the skin as an organ of (inter)subjectivity. In this chapter, the strange sensation of racialization guided me to use my own feeling body as a source of insight into how power relations are somatically encoded in the body. The strange sensation of racialization—the feelings of bodily dissonance, immobility, or displacement—signals the penetrating influence of race on one's embodied subjectivity. At the same time, it also reminds me of the ongoing and ceaseless presence of my feeling, moving, living body that absorbs, registers, and feels the forces, textures, movements, and sensations of racialization. Bodily sensations of racialization reveal both the forces of social inscription *and* the mortal presence of the body as a foundation of subjectivity. The living flesh of our bodies always defies the closure of meaning attempted by racialization.

The body is not an afterthought or even a product of social process; the lived body is always already perceptive, sensitive, and interactive with and within the social and material worlds. At the very core, race is a political tool of social organization and division—its very power lies in de-sensorializing our faces, bodies, and intercorporeal connections. In fighting racism, then, it only makes sense to re-sensorialize and reclaim our bodies—not as what we "possess" but as a condition in which—and because of which—our lived experiences are made possible. The narratives of race and racism must be told not from the "grid" of identity positioning, but from the multisensorial event of dynamic interaction and movement.[51] My primary concern in this chapter was not about my identity as Asian, but how the experience of racialization puts my body in motion into a particular flow of interpersonal encounters with others and intrapersonal relationship with my own embodiment. What being and becoming Asian feels like illuminates the excess and movements of our fleshy body that is always already more than what racialization and racism attempt to foreclose. The somatic sensations of racialization signal both the materiality of racialization that turns our bodies into an object, and the excess and movements of our fleshy bodies-as-subject that defy and leak through such objectification.

4

Sensing in Motion
The Kinesthetic Feelings of Race

Put yourself in this scenario for a moment. You and your partner are teaching a friend how to drive a car in an empty parking lot in Albuquerque, New Mexico. Your friend slowly drives the car forward while carefully making right and left turns at your request. You feel so comfortable and confident that you ask your friend to exit the lot, make a right turn onto the street, and drive to your partner's house. Suddenly, you hear your partner yell "What?!" from the backseat of the car, but you quickly retort "she is already a good driver." There is a brief moment of silence—some uncertainty creeps in and triggers doubt, but you instruct your friend to make the right turn, anyway. Your friend drives slowly in the right lane of one of Albuquerque's busiest streets. As your friend drives at a snail's pace, you observe the adobe multistory homes and murals abound. You feel the heat from the climate of the arid Southwest on your elbow and forearm as your right arm hangs and dangles like windswept leaves from the car's window. You give further instructions, "Now, I want you to focus on the car in front of you and maintain enough distance so that you can stop if necessary. Good! Now, I want you to take a quick look at the cars behind you in the left and center mirror. Pay attention to their movements. Good! You are doing well."

Your partner sits quietly in the backseat. You know that she is nervous. Your friend moves to the left lane and makes a left turn on to a one-way, single lane road toward your partner's neighborhood—described by some as the "student ghetto." You often smirk when you hear this reference since this neighborhood looks or feels nothing like the rough and tumble ones you know of in Chicago. It's a quiet evening and there are neither people nor cars in sight, so you ask your friend to slowly make the sharp left turn into your partner's driveway.

The confused look on your friend's face suddenly unnerves you; your friend quickly proceeds, turns the steering wheel too early and sharply, and you all instantaneously hear a high-pitched screeching sound underneath the car colliding with the sharp angle of the concrete curb of the sidewalk. You, your partner, and friend quickly jump out of the car to check for damage. You all observe the left front wheel of the car on the top of the curb, while the right front wheel and the two back wheels are situated in the street within the on-coming traffic. You immediately get into the car, shift the gear in reverse, and press the gas slightly to remove the front left wheel from the sidewalk. You expeditiously but safely drive the car onward and make the sharp turn into your partner's driveway. You get out of the car to check the front wheel and see that there is no visible damage. Your partner is a bit shaken—hearing the loud screeching sound underneath the car scraping against the pavement induces uneasiness in her.

Your partner and friend stand near the car for a couple of minutes as you bend down with a small flashlight in your hand to look for any signs of damage underneath the car. Since there is no visible damage, you all go inside the house. After some anxiety-ridden reflection mixed with sounds of nervous laughter, you all sit down to eat dinner. The smell of the spices in, and taste of, the hot ramen noodles put your partner and friend at ease while you reconcile asking your friend to make such a difficult turn because there were no people walking along the sidewalk. While slurping the hot noodles, you all, out of the blue, hear a loud knock on the door. The intensity of the sound jolts your partner and friend as they slightly leap upon hearing the loud knock. Yet, the brisk and frequent pounding is familiar to your ear—like someone vigorously pounding a nail with a hammer. It is the police knock—a loud, rapid, and incessant bang on the door that moves your body in ways that causes you to lose your normal, relaxed posture inducing a panic that heightens your senses not only to a police presence but also to the act of policing. The tactile speed of the officer's hand hitting the door and auditory reverberation of the knock prompt a fear-inducing stimuli that consumes and touches your body—a kinesthetic-tactile sensation stemming from a shiver that quickly touches and moves down your spine as you know this knock is a familiar signifier of a potential racialized encounter with police. Suddenly, the smell of the spices of hot ramen noodles dissipates, vanquished by grim and solemn memories of your experiences with police officers. But fear enhances your perception, moving through and touching various organs within your body as you are multisensorially consumed with a sharp focus in feeling the touch of the fear-eliciting knock.

Instantaneously, the sound of the knock curbs and pulls you as you move swiftly to answer the door—you know that police officers become more anxious when they have to wait even for a couple of seconds. You open the door and just as you deduced, there are three police officers, two males and one female, standing in the doorway. One of the male officers, who appears to be the eldest and in charge, stands in front of the other two officers. As he looks into your eyes, you fiddle with the small flashlight that you used earlier to look under the car. But, you are so transfixed on the navy blue uniform of the male officer, standing with his hands touching his hips while prominently displaying the handle of the gun in his hostler, that you didn't realize that the light from your flashlight is shining brightly in his face. He squints attempting to see through the glare of the light that touches his eyes, and demands, "Get that light out of my face." Without even turning off the flashlight or uttering a word, you drop it on the floor—you open your hand so quickly that you distinctly hear the "ping" sound as it hits the floor. Your experiences have taught you to make very simple and transparent movements when being approached by a police officer—limiting the use of your hands and immediately freeing them of any objects. These perceptions are primarily of a sensorial and kinesthetic self-awareness deriving from personal experiences, stories, and anecdotes on policing. Calling upon these memories allows you to sense, predict, and feel the spatial and temporal flow of the interbodily relations at stake when this very moment is sensually experienced.[1]

Despite these memories, you give fate a chance and roll the dice, so to speak. You believe that this circumstance might be different so you let your sensory guards down. The dark-blue night sky situated above the police officers' heads makes you feel unruffled, so you presume that they came to check if everyone is unharmed. But, before you utter a word, the officer says, "A neighbor said that you all got into an accident." You respond, "Accident! No one was harmed. There was no damage. We were just teaching our friend how to drive but she turned the steering wheel too early and the front left wheel ended up on the curb. I put the car in reverse, removing the wheel from the curb, and drove it into the driveway. She has a driver's permit and we have licenses." You immediately take heed to your bodily sensory inputs and outputs, allowing you to materially become conscious of your senses and feel the affective state of this encounter. In everyday interactions, you unconsciously use multiple hand gestures, shoulder shrugs, and facial expressions to complement your verbal communication, to be sure, and yet you are conscious of your bodily movements in this circumstance—you stand erect and make minimal gestures or movements with your hands holding them still to your side, touching your pants ever so slightly, so that they are visible to the officers. You also relax your facial muscles and make direct eye contact with the officer. Your eyes perceive these surroundings, and yet tactile and auditory sensations emerge quite prominently through the process of sensing the speed, rhythm, and intonations of the moving bodies and the forces that move them.

You are so focused on making direct eye contact that you observe the police officer's eye movements, darting quickly around the room, toward your partner and friend, and back to you. The speed, rhythm, and controlled movements of this officer's pupils suggest that his suspicions are aroused. The police officer then states, "Ok, everyone come outside." You are a bit confused but you walk outside with the two male police officers. It is dark so you all stand near a lit area near the house. You look back inside the house and notice that the female police officer waits to watch your partner and friend put on their shoes. Since the interaction starts without very strong emotions, you continue to explain while pointing toward the car that after you turned into the driveway, you "checked the front wheel, found no damage, and . . ." The officer, at once, interrupts by yelling, "Shut up and stay right here!" Your body stiffens in responding to the command and sudden change in the officer's tone. You are stunned. You feel this tingling sensation moving in your stomach. The piercing and contemptuous stare of his eyes touch your eyes for a few seconds, and you feel the gruff sound of his voice vigorously touch your stomach like a punch to the gut—halting any movement or flexibility of your limbs. He then moves to the aperture of the doorway, raises his hand, palm upward, and moves his index finger repeatedly motioning and beckoning toward your friend while saying, "You, come here, now." He tells the other male officer to "wait with [you]." You remain standing next to the cop that was assigned to you and slowly shake your head, sensing that this circumstance will soon intensify. Experience has taught you so much—you know the drill after a few unnecessary stop-and-frisk searches. The somatosensory feedback and reactions trigger conscious bodily senses and sensations associated with other intense emotional experiences. You sense the proprioceptive input, those sensations in the muscles and joints in your body that you feel when you negotiate the space between your anger and the actions of others. Yet, you have a kinesthetic sense of how the *racial tensions* and acts of policing will mediate and control how your body moves and contorts with those of your partner, friend, and the police officers.

Suddenly, the bodies within this encounter move quickly, but the time and pace slow down for you. Again, experience has taught you so much about compulsory compliance with police. You turn in one direction and the male police officer, who just told you to "shut up," walks with your friend to the driveway and conducts a sobriety test. With the loud and low-pitched sound of the word "shut up" still ringing in your ears, you stand completely still but with your arms folded—as you tuck in your cheeks to swallow your saliva to keep your mouth moist. Your initial fears become anger. As you watch the officer conduct the field sobriety test, you shake your head in disgust. Like a doctor testing a patient's pupils, the cop points a flashlight into the eyes of your friend to see how they react to the light. Occasionally, you peer at the sloped pavement of the driveway to slow your heart rate and manage feelings of pain curtailing the anger triggered by not only this perceived provocation but also thoughts of past experiences. He stops from time to time to turn his eyes toward you. You muse that he feels threatened by your posture so you unfold your arms and slowly place your hands to your side—consciously avoiding your pockets. Again, you know that you must curb and balance the tension between movements of your posture, eyes, and facial expressions with that of the officer's eyes and his piercing gaze that frequently touches you.

You then turn your head in the other direction to check on your partner. While turning, you observe that the female police officer is in a *stand your ground* posture while placing her hand on her holster in search of her gun. She steps her front foot forward with the other foot directly behind, to anchor her body and possibly show dominance. She leans forward like a wide receiver standing at the line of scrimmage awaiting a quarterback to receive a football from the center lineman, and slightly raises her voice by saying, "Slowly, slowly, come on out now!" Your eyes widen in trauma. You cannot see your partner because she is still inside the house. She arrives to the entrance and you see her rush to twist her foot in a shoe. Your initial instinct is to yell, "Hey, why are you reaching for your gun? She is not a criminal!" But, as you start to open your mouth, you quickly close off the sound and words from coming out—you don't want to startle a perceptibly nervous police officer who is searching for a gun. You also know that the officer, who told you to "shut up" and occasionally stares at you, is ready to act. At the same time, you worry for your partner as the female officer's right hand stumbles over the buckle strap of the holster while probing for the gun handle. Later, you find out that this officer was reacting to the bodily movements of your partner who reached to turn off a small electric heater located under the coffee table. Still, you wonder why the female officer remains in her stance with her hand on the gun handle after seeing that your partner had neither weapon nor intention to cause any harm. You feel the rhythms of your and the officers' movements and know that any mistaken or sudden maneuvers may cause the police officers to act forcefully. So, you let your shoulders fall back and allow your arms to fall loosely at your sides to reduce the mounting tension in your body.

Still, you are confused and your thinking is muddled—while you know and have experienced how police officers act suspiciously toward you and people who look like you, your partner and friend are international students who never interacted with them in this way. You wonder what and how they are feeling. After your partner walks through the door safely, you turn to the police officer who stands nearby with both hands on his hips and in a quiet murmur state, "We are PhD students, not criminals; we didn't break the law." Suddenly the officer who appears to be almost done with the sobriety test hears you and yells, "Shut the fuck up or I will take you in." You are bewildered. Your body freezes and tenses upon hearing the command. You put your head down to avoid eye contact with the officer, but you could feel his eyes ripping through your skin while he glares, again, at you. Although "touching is not seeing," you still feel the force of the haptics of his eyes on your body.[2] Your stomach is queasy—churning like a machine that shakes whole milk to make butter. The haptics of his eyes and the acoustics of his voice cause your eyes to move and set in motion a nauseous sensation that flows through your body depriving you of any sense of humanity. Not only do you feel humiliated, but you feel like a coward. You believe that he will enact physical punishment on a whim. After the officer continues with the sobriety test, you lift your head and look at the officer standing nearest you. He catches your eye, shrugs his shoulders, and gestures with his left hand toward his partner. You sense in seeing his lowered eyebrows and scrunched lips that he knows that these actions are excessive but he has to follow the orders of the superior officer. There is something sensuously palpable between you and this police officer standing nearest you—an interkinesthetic comportment involving a heightened sensitivity to sensations of hearing, the touching eye, or feeling with muscles and joints where you both experience a particular act of policing.[3]

After finding that your friend is not inebriated, the male police officer calls you over and shouts, "She almost hit a pedestrian!" You wonder, first, why he came to you and second, you are wary of his motives since there were no pedestrians on the street during that time. But, you know that he wants you to give him a reason to put you on the ground, handcuff you, and throw you in the backseat of the police car, so you remain silent standing with your arms touching the side of your pants and with your eyes focused on the walkway. You just listen and slightly use your gym shoe to smooth some loose aggregation of gravel. The sound and gruff tone from the officer saying "shut the fuck up" still rings in your ears, so you know and feel that he wants to start trouble. You slightly lift your head and look toward the ground—he senses your obedience by the way you move your head and your untouched eyes so he reasserts his dominance. He moves his body closer to you and glares down on to your head waiting for you to say anything. You feel his eyes on top of your head as you look toward the ground. Here, you experience an unpleasant distressing feeling move through your body, but your body movements conceal your pain as you detach your gaze, and smooth the gravel with your foot. Your jaw still wobbles in anger. You feel like a child being reprimanded by a parent. You have neither power nor voice, so you capitulate by nodding your head and saying, "We apologize, we will be more careful." The police officer nods his head but you remain quiet. You keep your eyes toward the ground—feeling humiliated and angry—but you just want them to leave. Even as the officer turns to leave, you still feel like his hateful eyes are affixed on top of your head. The officers walk away, but not before the police officer who stood next to you for the entire time kindly says, "Take care, man." Your hunch about him was probably correct.

You walk inside of the house and your partner says, "What just happened?" Your friend responds by apologizing. You promptly grit your teeth and throw a punch in the air, seeking to retrieve your body and escape the psychological and kinesthetic hold of it by the police officer. You want to release the pent up emotions of anger, frustration, shame, and fear, so you vigorously express, "You shouldn't have to apologize! That was so unnecessary. I hated that!" Your friend looks subdued and exhausted and, in fact, almost numb. She, again, in a quiet tone, apologizes to your partner. You wonder if she is conscious of, or even heard your fit-of-anger. You turn to your partner who is still somewhat shaken from hearing the screeching sound of the pavement under her car. In trying to square the confusing bedlam of emotions, she states, "Why did you tell her to make that turn?" You reply, "I thought that she could make it because she was driving so well. It was sharp turn, but we checked everything. The car was fine, and it wasn't an accident." But that's neither here nor there so you ask her, "Did you see the female cop reach for her gun like she was going to shoot you?" Your partner sits without response. At this moment, you start to mine the meanings of this circumstance for them. You feel like they are desensitized to what just happened. You wonder why they didn't share your deep emotions. Why are they now worried about the car when we moved on from it? You feel like this genuinely illuminating encounter only fostered feelings of guilt and remorse rather than injustice in them. You finally realize that your partner and friend don't experience the world in the same way that you do. Their bodies have never appeared to be a *threat* to, or been put in motion by, the police. But yours has.

About ten years later, you, your partner, and friend reflect back on this moment. After living in the United States for some time, your partner and friend have come to see various newsworthy events involving police harassment and shootings. In fact, they both speak frankly about how they were oblivious of the magnitude of these police officers' actions. To be sure, your partner states with real fear in her voice, "At the time, I didn't know that reaching for a button to turn off an electric heater was threatening. She could have shot me!" You respond, "It should not have gone that far!"

Sensing and Feeling Racism in Motion

After pondering this incident, a series of what-ifs, facilitating the kinesthetic expressions, the sensory modalities, and somatosensory feedback immediately come to mind. What if you had neither kinesthetic awareness nor firsthand emotional memories of encounters with police officers? What if that shiver moving down your spine doesn't prompt these memories? What if you made other moves with the flashlight instead of just dropping it? What if you raised your voice and clutched your fists to vehemently repudiate the officer's claim that you all were involved in an accident and suggest that your friend was well within her legal right to refuse a field sobriety test? What if your friend drank a can of beer or a glass of wine while in the house, precipitating a misguided judgment that she was inebriated while driving? What if the female officer was able to grab her gun while observing your partner's attempt to turn off a heater? Then again, what if you yelled, "Why are you reaching for your gun, don't shoot my partner" startling the female officer who was already in a stand your ground posture? What if the officer, who stands next to you, decries the actions of his fellow officers? What if you engaged in kinesthetic behaviors undermining the officer's authority such as fiercely glaring into his eyes, placing your hands into your pockets, or gesturing uncontrollably in ways that would elevate the tension? Then again, what if you acted arrogantly, suppressing the touch of the sick, fear-inducing feeling in your stomach? What if you reproached the officer who told you to "shut the fuck up" reacting angrily to the high-pitch volume of the command by moving toward the police officer? What if you refuted, "You are lying, there were no passersby" when the officer stated that you all almost hit a pedestrian? What if you had no way of releasing the kinesthetic hold that the officer had over you after the incident? What if your partner and friend would have reacted differently with the knowledge that they currently have about policing? What if it were daylight and the temperatures were unseasonably hot or cold? Suddenly, you realize that a single false or misunderstood move—any number of misconstrued behaviors, oversights, or misdirected emotional outbursts carried out within the frame of these "what-ifs"—would have possibly changed you, your partner, and friend's life forever.

Depending on your racial background perhaps you might feel or sense this experience quite differently. If you are white, you may struggle to engage and reconcile some of the sensory input and output within this story. In fact, you may see this as an isolated incident or exaggerated account. Surely, studies show that police officers treat and speak to whites with more respect than blacks during traffic stops and other situations.[4] If you are black, you may identify with this story at the somatosensory level. This experience may summon your own memories of police violence or harassment, not only as it occurred but also as it was felt in and through your body. You also know that blacks frequently lament unjust practices in high-profile cases of police misconduct or use of excessive force.[5] To be sure, this vignette is a true account of an experience of policing involving me, an African American male, who is the *you* in this story, *your partner* who is actually the coauthor of this book and is a Japanese female, and *your friend*, who is the driver of the car and is also a Japanese female. The police officers in this encounter are all Caucasian. Pairing *you* with the narration of my first-person point of view gives you a peek into the memories, emotions, and sensory perceptions of a black man who works through some of the complexities of policing. In highlighting the interplay between my body and embodied forms of communication, I welcome you to experience the kinesthetic feelings of this racialized encounter through my body, facilitating the haptics of my eyes with those of the police officer's, the forceful sound of the officer's voice managing my bodily motions and movements, and the haptics of the police knock on the door pulling me readily toward the door. The racial sensorium forms particular kinds of vulnerability and immobility, in which people of color must manage or remain alert to the very misjudgments, misinterpretations, or racist operations while fearing that their bodies can be, unjustly, taken at any moment.

Bodily experience is a complex, generally unconscious process involving the coordination of diverse sensory inputs and information—primarily visual, proprioceptive, physiognomic, and motor systems. The body, too, carries a reflexive capacity, a way of reacting to the world by how "we sense ourselves sensing the world."[6] The embodiment and control of one's body is a seemingly negligible dimension of the self that is nevertheless essential for managing interactions with people and even external objects. To be sure, Maurice Merleau-Ponty's phenomenological project compels us to see that all bodies *can* seamlessly extend themselves to act in various situations.[7] As Simone de Beauvoir once asserted in citing Merleau-Ponty, my body "is not a thing, it is a situation: it is [my] grasp on the world."[8] Yet a reading of the kinesthetic feelings of racialized body schemas alongside an analyses of sensory assemblages uniquely highlights how people of color *must* coordinate the movement of their bodies, involuntarily, to the movements of whites for fear that at any moment their body could be seized or extracted without repercussion. In particular, the history of colonialism shapes all bodies, subjecting people of color to become subjects incapable of acting and putting objects to use. That is, race is a bodily given such that all bodies are "bodily extensions of [white people]."[9] As Fanon once asserted, "The white gaze, the only valid one, is already dissecting me. I am fixed. Once their microtomes are sharped, the whites objectively cut sections of my reality."[10] In fleshing out the kinesthetic feelings of race, the preceding sensory narrative[11] showed how an involuntary, coercive, shared, and lateral sense-formation develops from feelings of inferiority and fears of difference in this intercorporeal encounter between me, my partner, and friend, and the law enforcement officers. The sensory narrative provided a means for exploring the senses to understand racialized experiences, and of capturing these experiences as not only embodied but inscribed in social meanings of race. Race, in this instance, is *sensed* or *felt* when being black calls for experiencing movements that result in the loss of agency and feelings of helplessness at the corporeal level.

Allow me now to elaborate on the sensations of the kinesthetic feelings in considering the movement of bodies within this perceptibly racist (or internalized racist) encounter in foregrounding its affectivity. The notion of affectivity, here, "emphasizes something that is sensuously palpable, yet already permeated with affective tone . . . already involving the experiencer's kinesthetic capability for receptivity and response."[12] My awareness of interkinesthetic behaviors is one in which my movements are predicated on verbal commands and kinesthetic feelings that are, indeed, a part of the racial sensorium. The kinesthetic feelings of racism are felt and sensed here in the same way that interpersonal encounters develop in the medium of interkinesthetic affectivity[13]—a sensibility for perceiving the postures, movements, and felt bodily sensations that cause me to recoil, calibrate, and contort my body and affectively in response to the white racist gaze of the police officer who is suspicious of my presence as a black man. It is my body that becomes this movable object where I lose, give, and relinquish control to the somatosensory systems of whiteness.

First, the conscious process of proprioception provides us with knowledge of the intersubjective forces that direct, (re)position, and control our body. We not only give, receive, and feel kinesthetic messages from others[14] but also are aware of how our bodies are positioned and moved in concert with others. By way of illustration, while one may causally conceive of the body as abstracted from movement, its anticipatory motions in this interplay works with multiple sensations of which I frequently feel vulnerable in the presence of police officers. I felt the tactile sensations of my eyes moving downward in the direction of the ground, feeling on my skin the touch of the police officer's piercing eyes. The chilling skin sensation caused by his stare immobilized me, making it very hard to attend to the sensations of the deep ache and nausea in my stomach and quivering hands. I further felt immobilized in hearing the police officer's low-pitched tones expressing, "Shut the fuck up or I will take you in" together with his slow movement toward me. As his glare ripped through my skin, the sound of this degrading and threatening command penetrated and moved through my body making my stomach turn and feel queasy. I feared that the worst was yet to come—further debasement or even physical harm that I did not want to feel or experience. Thus, these sequences of movements (including placing my hands to my side while intentionally avoiding my pockets) evinced the vulnerability that I felt, which took away any sense or feelings of agency in me. If I responded otherwise with bodily movements such as placing my hands in my pockets or tarrying my eyes to him, he probably would have moved quickly to physically assert his dominance by throwing me to the ground or handcuffing me. Since I am aware of the stereotypical perceptions of violent and uncontrolled black masculinity, I attempted to dispel these white supremacist perceptions by monitoring my body and allowing the police officer to have a kinesthetic hold and control over it. The fact that I recognized and responded to my own vulnerability, quickly processed my own past experiences, and moved along with the posture, bodily positions, and verbal commands of the police officers, showed how my own understanding of racial tensions of policing have trained me to be intuitively engaged with the assemblage of haptic-aural, haptic-visual, kinesics-optics, and tactile-kinesthetic sensations of racist encounters with law enforcement.

Second, the proprioception as well as kinesthetic feelings of race developed a bodily timidity, which came from experiences—occurring in the physical and mental processes of recollection or through a "knowledge-embodied process"[15]—of having my body, regularly, regulated and moved as an object of the sensory modalities of whiteness. Consider, for example, the moment that the police officer quickly and loudly pounds on my partner's door. The abrupt, frequent, and intense sound and tactile sensation of the police knock undoubtedly provided somatosensory feedback that alerted and moved the bodies of my partner, friend, and me. The auditory stimulus startled my partner and friend triggering an involuntary movement or a reflex in their head and shoulders. Yet the loud sound and intense tactile banging on the door produced immediate movements of shivering sensations that touched my spine, and set in motion memories of my experiences of being approached by law enforcement.

While my partner and friend sat still, my ears perked up to the sound of the police knock. I felt pulled toward the door by the racist rope of the loud and tactile police knock. As I raced to the door, I felt a compelling unity between the movement of my body—my legs and arms moving quickly—and the tactile speed and sound of the police knock. It was as if my bodily movement, the officer's hand, and the banging noise coordinated with one another—unfolding events that repeatedly ingrains the somatic rules of how bodies move, feel, and occupy space in interactions between law enforcement officers and civilians of color in the United States. Racist ideologies of the police knock, not only underpin what I know, think, or act in hearing it but also produce somatic knowledge replete with kinesthetic feelings of racism—the tactile, loud bang of the police knock signifying a police presence, immediately, codes and signals that my bodily movements are about to be forcefully regulated.

Finally, interdependent bodies attune to the rhythms and pace of intersubjective forces producing kinesthetic feelings that induce fear, immobility, and subservience. Consider the moment when the white female officer moves her body in the *stand your ground* posture. She coordinates multiple sensory inputs and outputs, and moves into this posture in fear of the threat of my partner's kinesthetic behavior of potentially reaching for a weapon. The loud, slow annunciations of the officer stating "slowly, slowly, come on out now" and the officer's hand movements of fidgeting for her gun induces my partner to move quickly to the doorway. They both understand and perceive the world and one another in unique ways precipitating a sequence of interactions that unfold as they react to each other's bodily movements. For instance, my partner normally turns off the space heater to conserve energy when she leaves the house. Since her body has never been viewed as a threat by police officers, she could not anticipate that this officer would react in fear of sudden movements in leaning downward to turn off the space heater with her hand. But, the police officer panicked and perhaps felt some distress in searching for the gun in considering my partner's movements as a threat to her. The embodied feedback loops of interkinesthetic sensorial reciprocity facilitate how they coordinate or orient their body movements in response to each other's actions. The police officer's command as she moved her hand to reach for her gun produced a gesture of compliance in my partner who coordinated her bodily movements in rushing quickly to put on her shoes in response. This interaction is not simply a fleeting moment between my partner and this female police officer; it is historically rooted and rehearsed in white racial performance and framings of people of color who are to be feared due to their perceived and stereotyped criminal inclinations.

Conclusion

In his book *Black Bodies, White Gazes*, George Yancy modifies Fanon's phenomenology of blackness to show how the powerful white objectifying gaze surveils and shapes the behaviors, attitudes, and is even implicated in the oppression of blacks.[16] Yancy claimed that the corporeal integrity of the black body is subjected to a process of self-doubt, self-alienation, and self-hatred because the white gaze "confiscated [it] within social spaces of meaning construction."[17] Fanon alluded to this sense of being controlled and exploited when he spoke of unexpected interactions with white people or, more fittingly, when he perceived, sensed, and felt the force of the white gaze on his otherized body.[18] In his best-selling book *Between the World and Me*,[19] Ta-Nehisi Coates pays homage to James Baldwin's 1963 classic book, *The Fire Next Time*, by writing an epistolary memoir that narrates the experiences and perils of the black body and subjectivity living under the gun, so to speak.[20] Like Baldwin, who writes a letter to his fifteen-year-old nephew to awaken him to his own black humanity, Coates writes a letter to his son, Samori, explaining how he must properly comport himself in white America despite living with a plundered black body that suffers from cruel realities of the American Dream.[21] Growing up with a black body is terrifying for Coates; he fears for his body and his son's body—a fear fostered through the betrayals of criminal justice system in failing to convict police officers in the killing of unarmed black people like Trayvon Martin, Freddie Gray, Michael Brown, Eric Garner, Tamir Rice, Renisha McBride, and his schoolmate Prince Jones. Like Yancy, Coates's approach is similar in prose to Fanon's[22] in conjoining the racial politics of nation-states and history with embodied layers of black subjection and subjugation.

The phenomenology of the body is a necessary starting point to consider its varied physical sensations shaping, managing, and controlling the way people of color interact with white people in the world. This is to say that our subjectivity is never divorced from the world, and cannot be understood apart of its dynamic, lived, and embodied experience.[23] Case in point, Coates's idée fixe with a phenomenology of the black body demonstrates how the black body in the United States, historically, has collapsed under the gaze of white people.[24] As Coates once proclaimed, "The plunder of black life was drilled into [the United States] in its infancy and reinforced across its history, so that plunder has become an heirloom, an intelligence, a sentience, a default setting to which, likely to the end of our days, we must invariably return."[25] Coates, quite uniquely, views black disembodiment as the accumulated legacies and circumstances of plundering that has taken a psychological and physical toll on the mobility of black bodies, including the slave trade, plantation economy, the convict leasing system, penal labor, hyper-incarceration, lynching, stop-and-frisk, shopping while black, and police harassment and brutality.[26] This leads Coates to assert that freedom stops short of an embrace of racial progress, but requires grappling with the psychic paralysis of helplessness and social immobility as the historical condition of black people. Coates thus knows that the psyche or the very soul of black folks is not entirely theirs.[27]

What distinguishes Merleau-Ponty's or other Western phenomenology of the body from Coates's refrains and Fanon's phenomenology of the black body is that both Fanon and Coates perceive the body as shaped within *historicity*. Although the sensorial and emotional dimensions of human behavior are culturally constructed, they are constituted in our experiences and in history.[28]

Reflexivity of our embodied somatosensory impulses ceases to restrict emotions and perhaps adds clarity to the material and physical domains of subjectivity that form our racialized experiences. As embodied beings, our experience of our body is habitually pre-reflective, which takes on a reflective self-consciousness once we take on a conceptual, explicit, and subjective awareness of how it coordinates and orients with other beings or apparatuses. It is through our sensing and sensed body that we come to understand and perceive how our bodies are not purely conceived with agency to exist freely, but are situated physically and spatially within the context of the past and present. Like the black slave who had to master the averted and downward look or direct their gaze, obsequiously, toward their white slave owner within volatile white supremacist institutions, blacks, who are often victims of various forms of covert and overt oppression, learn to negotiate, organize, and control kinesthetic and somatosensory behaviors in a racist society.

Many scholars discuss a litany of public encounters where African Americans articulate and draw on their own experiences of aggressive policing in their communities.[29] The production of suspicious black bodies, not as objects of fear, but of phobic horror becomes real in the racist gaze that marks black bodies as suspicious in the racial profiling operative in the enforcement of "stop-and-frisk" policies or when George Zimmerman fatally shot Trayvon Martin, a seventeen-year-old African American teenager because he looked like a "suspicious" character who appeared to be "up to no good." Yet, perceived acts of policing facilitated particular kinesthetic feelings, or alterations in my body with overpowering psychic feelings of black subjection. That is, my vulnerability and fears resulted in bodily movements that made me feel restrained and immobile to the actions of these police officers. These interkinesthetic moments produced particular sensations in which I experienced my movements without feeling any sense of agency. Perhaps emotions of fear, frustration, and anger induce black bodies to move or inhibit movement in certain ways because such micro bodily movements take place within the larger history of white supremacy. Historically, these bodily movements charged with emotions have been rehearsed in response to the violence of white supremacy and acquiescent contortions of the black body in the United States. The kinesthetic feelings of race and racism, specifically, invade the sensory modalities of black people—infiltrating the somatosensory system and seizing on the body's vulnerability, interdependence, and mobility in ways that make one feel and experience a momentarily loss of the self in fearing that their body will be physically and psychologically taken away at any moment.

5

A Phenomenology of the Racialized Tongue

Embodiment, Language, and the Bodies That Speak

In his discussion of speech act theory, John L. Austin theorized the performativity of linguistic utterances that function as a form of action rather than simply describing or making statements about reality.[1] In this view, speaking is a social act through which we accomplish certain material, relational, and political effects and consequences. Judith Butler developed the notion of performativity further by analyzing gender as a stylized repetition of social acts that produce material, gendered, and sexed bodies.[2] Implicit in Butler's view of performativity is the idea that we become that which we do through bodily engagements with the world. If Austin asked about the performativity of speech (how we *do* things with words) and Butler the performativity of gendered acts (how we *do* gender), in this chapter we address the performative effects of the act of speaking in constituting the speaking subject. The act of speaking is a form of stylized repetition of social acts. Beyond (or aside from) the symbolic meaning of uttered words, the act of speaking "properly" and "intelligibly" is a process of disciplining the body and materializing a certain kind of body. In the cultural matrices of power and hegemony, how do we emerge as embodied communicative subjects through the act of speaking? How do we sense and feel the process of speaking and becoming a certain type of speaking subject?

As speakers of English as a second language and dialect, we find it particularly interesting to explore the bodily experiences of speaking as a communicative phenomenon of its own. Sachi grew up in Japan and learned to speak SAE in her late teens, while Chris grew up navigating between Black English Vernacular (BEV) in his neighborhood in Chicago and SAE in his public and private education. For the both of us, speaking SAE is never a neutral act; our acts of speaking are loaded with social and ideological implications associated with certain types of cultural performance (i.e., sense of belonging, demonstration of cultural membership, assimilation, and performance of intelligence). Our embodied experiences of disciplining our bodies to speak a second language and dialect draw us into interrogating the performativity of bodily acts of speaking as communicative subjects. What interests us is not the "what" of speech, but the "how" of speaking, the act of speaking itself.

We approach the act of speaking as habituated embodiment, resulting from an orchestration of vocal, auditory, and sensorimotor experiences within a particular system of cultural and ideological practice.[3] The act of speaking is ideological not only because of the symbolic content of speech but more fundamentally because it materially and kinesthetically engages the body based on culturally established rules and norms. We interrogate the constitutive moments when one's speech coheres as a historically situated and physically orchestrated action, illuminating the act of speaking as a fundamental process of becoming an embodied communicative subject. By focusing on the tongue as a sensuous organ of identity expression and negotiation, we demonstrate how racialized subjectivities are felt and sensed through the somatic labor of *speaking-almost-white-but-not-quite*.

In the following, we first situate our discussion within the larger scholarly conversations on communication, embodiment, and performativity. Second, we establish our theoretical perspective on the act of speaking as habituated embodiment using insights from Pierre Bourdieu and Maurice Merleau-Ponty.[4] We then focus on the intersection between the act of speaking and racial embodiment by using the notion of mimicry introduced by Homi K. Bhabha.[5] Third, we provide our phenomenological descriptions, describing and analyzing our acts of disciplining our bodies to speak SAE as embodied, material processes of becoming within the complex matrices of racialized power and social relations.[6] We conclude by addressing the significance of bodily enactment and habituation in constituting a particular communicative subject, highlighting and complicating the materiality of power in which the enactive body serves as a disciplinary device to remember, preserve, legitimate, and/or resist the hegemonic ways of being-in-the-world.[7] Resisting the approach that the body is a socially constructed textual surface on which meanings are inscribed and negotiated, we call for a more phenomenological and sensorial understanding of the body and embodiment in communication.

Communication, Performativity, and Embodiment

At the core of our theoretical inquiry is the question about the role of the body and embodiment in communication theorizing. Various scholars have theorized and politicized communicative acts as embodied and performative practice, focusing on the materiality of lived bodies in constituting meaning, identity, knowledge, and experience. The underlying perspective in communication as embodied practice is that the body is more than a surface of symbolic inscription. Social ideologies and cultural hegemony become materialized through the body's enactive capacity and reiterative bodily performance.[8]

For example, John T. Warren and Amy K. Kilgard use the notion of "enfleshing whiteness" in order to make visible how whiteness is performatively accomplished and constituted through the "embodied enactment" of racial identity.[9] Similarly, Bryant Keith Alexander and John T. Warren use Peter McLaren's notion of "enfleshed knowledge" to deconstruct how cultural differences and relations of power are incorporated into the subject's corporeality, particularly in educational contexts.[10] In critiquing superficial analyses of intersectional identity as "disembodied knowledge," Gust A. Yep coined the term "thick intersectionalities" to attend to "the lived experiences and biographies of the persons occupying a particular intersection of various identity positions, including how they inhabit and make sense of their own bodies."[11]

A focus on embodiment allows scholars to address the bodily felt dimensions of identity politics. Julie-Ann Scott provides a compelling account of the social and ideological implications of how we become who we are through bodily ways of knowing and bodily capacities of doing.[12] Claudio Moreira and Marcelo Diversi argue that the work of decolonizing academic spaces must begin by theorizing about visceral experiences of everyday oppression and discrimination.[13] We join these ongoing theoretical explorations into the question of the body and embodiment in communication by concentrating on the act of speaking as a performative enactment.

The act of speaking requires a body that speaks—that does the speaking— not as an innate capacity, but as an outcome of social cultivation and ideological contouring. Revealing itself as a contested site where social and ideological forces inevitably clash with the biological and material, the act of uttering sounds into coherent words and structured sentences involves something deeply bodily, material, and enactive. We use the term "enactive" to connote that rather than simply being constituted biologically or constructed socially, the body is an active constructor of action, experience, and meaning. There is also something bodily laborious about being "articulate" and "intelligible" in verbal exchanges with others, especially in a cultural context that is not one's own. By describing how we bring our bodies into the intentional, existential act of speaking English as a second language and dialect, we theorize the materiality of a speaking body and its performative effects on being and becoming a communicative subject. Theorizing the act of speaking as a process of embodying a particular cultural self, in which the existential act of speaking intersects with the hegemonic influence of being spoken into a cultural/racial subject, we foreground the sensuous materiality of the body in understanding how cultural and ideological bodies come to matter.

The Act of Speaking as Habituated Embodiment

"A habit is *a continuation of willing that no longer needs to be willed*."[14]

In developing our conceptual framework, we approach speaking as a form of habituated embodiment—not only in terms of its culturally specific significations of gestures, accents, or mannerisms but more fundamentally in terms of its bodily engagement and stylization in the movement of the mouth and tongue, the rhythm of breathing, and the vocal production and auditory absorption of sounds. In the act of speaking, we not only produce symbolic meaning but also orchestrate our bodily movements, perceptions, and actions into communicative bodies. Emphasizing the centrality of the body in the act of speaking, Merleau-Ponty states, "The body converts a certain motor essence into vocal form, spreads out the articulatory style of a word into audible phenomena, and arrays the former attitude, which is resumed, into the panorama of the past, projecting an intention to move into actual movement, because the body is a power of natural expression."[15]

Rather than simply producing noise, the act of speaking crystallizes at the intersection of specific physiopsychological functions and the culturally specific cultivation of such functions. Both enactive and enacted, the speaking body manifests willed behavior and cultural codes—not only speaking ideas into being but also emerging into a body that speaks a given language. In this sense, not only do we become that which we speak *about* (discursive construction of reality/identity) but we also become the language we speak (sensory embodiment). In his discussion on *habitus*, Bourdieu argues that cultural norms and values gain a hegemonic and durable presence when cultural subjects are able to coordinate their actions and behaviors with historically constituted, external structures of culture without explicit awareness or conscious efforts.[16] Following Bourdieu, it can be viewed that speaking is a culturally habituated act through which individuals incorporate and internalize the objective structures of culture into their bodies. Such objective structures of culture may manifest in grammatical structures of a certain language, relational hierarchies embedded in linguistic expressions, or nonverbal codes that regulate interpersonal interactions. Thus, when small children learn how to speak a language, it is a bodily, physically enactive process through which "history [is] turned into nature" and cultural principles are remembered through their bodily enactments of speaking.[17] Far from being natural or neutral, the constitution of a habituated body both ensures and hides the unnatural history of crafting certain communicative subjects. Thus, the act of speaking constitutes a particular habitus; it regulates patterns of behavior, while leaving open improvisational and generative possibilities of speaking.

Through our habituated act of speaking, we also construct a particular habitus in a surrounding social space. For example, the use of eye contact (or the lack thereof) in different cultural contexts speaks to the spatiality of communicative engagements in which we gauge and define our physical, social, and emotional distance among speakers via the act of looking into each other's eyes. Speaking creates a particular acoustic cultural environment that can make one feel at home, while alienating others. Extending the notion of speaking as embodiment, then, the act of speaking is a form of habituated spatial arrangement in which we extend our speaking bodies into space as surrounding spaces accommodate and afford, or resist, our culturally habituated bodily existences.

Mimicry and Racial Embodiment

The notion of mimicry reveals the ambivalence embedded in the constitution of self-other, colonizer-colonized, and white-nonwhite relations. Using the historical examples of European colonialism in colonies such as India and Africa, Bhabha claims that mimicry functions in both oppressive and subversive ways. On the one hand, colonizers try to "civilize" the colonized society according to the values and norms of their culture by instilling their presumed superiority into forming the subjectivities of the colonized. This "desire for a reformed, recognizable Other" is inherently ambivalent because the colonizer seeks "*a subject of a difference that is almost the same, but not quite.*"[18] The colonized subjects are cultivated into European subjectivity to the extent that they serve as bridges and translators between the colonizers and the colonized masses.

On the other hand, Bhabha contends, mimicry is subversive when "its slippage, its excess, [and] its difference" reveals the artificiality of European superiority.[19] Applying the notion of mimicry to the contemporary cultural politics of hip-hop, Liam Grealy argues that the performance of black hip-hop artists functions as a form of mimicry in the sense that they mimic not the colonizer, but "the colonizer's version of [themselves]."[20] The excessive self-portrayal of hypermasculinity, violence, misogyny, and wealth does not *represent* their reality; rather it *re-presents* white imaginations of black communities and invokes white anxiety and ambivalence toward the increased visibility and articulatory power of hip-hop generations.

When we approach the act of speaking as a form of embodiment, we must also attend to the fact that an individual embodies their race and ethnicity through speech. The notion of racial mimicry relates closely to the issues of language and cultural identity, and within the United States, speech patterns and styles are racially coded. The so-called SAE is a code word for "white" English with deeply embedded assumptions about intelligence, knowledge, truth, credibility, and authority.[21] For black children in inner-city schools, for example, "speaking white" carries connotations of racial betrayal as well as a promise for upward mobility in a white-dominated society.[22] Speaking white becomes a form of racial mimicry in which racialized others hybridize, incorporate, and internalize the hegemony of white speech, while subverting its dominance through the performance of almost the same, but not quite.[23]

Thus, the actual act of speaking almost-white-but-not-quite can be a contested site of racial performativity and embodiment. The regulated principles of white speech become visible when a racialized body fails to follow them. In the next section, we will briefly explain our methodological approach, followed by our personal accounts of disciplining our bodies to speak English as a second language and dialect.

Methodological Approach

We combine insights from phenomenology and autoethnography in order to account for our direct bodily experiences and embodied struggles to speak SAE as racialized subjects. On the one hand, we utilize phenomenology as a theoretical and methodological foundation to articulate how we subjectively experience the acts of disciplining our bodies to speak SAE.[24] We carefully describe what it is like to (try to) speak SAE, illuminating how our enactive and material bodies are orchestrated to enact/mimic normative ways of speaking in the United States.[25] On the other hand, using insights from autoethnography, we politicize our subjectively lived, embodied negotiations of speaking SAE. The autoethnographic approach pays attention to the historical, ideological, and political dimensions of personal experience.[26] In this sense, we view our habituated and disciplined acts of speaking as historically situated and ideologically constructed. Thus, we interrogate our subjective bodily experiences and habituated/disciplined embodiments as contested sites of re/production(s) of hegemonic power.

By drawing methodological insights from phenomenology and autoethnography, we strive for a "more visceral and materialized understanding of power" to interrogate our seemingly mundane "subjective experience itself as a contested site of the re/production of hegemonic power."[27] In our narratives, we seek to provide nuanced descriptions of our bodily enactments and our embodiments of multiple linguistic selves to contextualize and politicize how cultural structures and social ideologies become "enfleshed" and "incorporated" into our bodies, paying particular attention to how the site of ideological formation is not simply a rhetorical struggle over meaning, but also a habituated embodiment that often remains mundane and seemingly nonideological.

The Unruly Tongue: A Phenomenology of Speaking English as a Second language (Sachi)

When I speak English, I am not simply doing things with words—as Austin would claim—I am doing things with my breath, tongue, mouth, ears, and body in general.[28] As a native of Japan, learning how to speak SAE has been a process of re-habituating my bodily movements, senses, and perceptions within the larger context of global English hegemony.[29] It is a process of habituating my body and programming my behaviors according to what is "normal" and "appropriate" in social contexts of this particular language. The re-habituation of my body began, quite literally, with my tongue. When I was in high school in Japan, my English teacher would give us handouts with visual explanations of how to pronounce certain sounds in English—such as the sound of "L," "R," or "TH"—sounds that we do not use in Japanese. On the handout were simple drawings of a facial profile with varying placements of the tongue— gently touching the upper teeth, tucked in the mouth, or placed between lower and upper teeth. In class, students would repeat after the teacher as we listened to his pronunciations and shifted the locations of our tongues to produce similar sounds. To pronounce the "TH" sound, for example, we would place our tongue in between the lower and upper teeth and gently blow out the air. I struggled the most with pronouncing the "R" sound, feeling as if my tongue was not flexible enough and as if I was using a muscle that I never even knew existed before. Suddenly my tongue felt like an organism of its own, unwilling to conform to my command of action. Learning how to speak English has been as much about taming my tongue as learning new words and grammar. But perhaps this "taming" of the tongue is integral to learning a language, whether it is one's primary or secondary language. Learning a second language makes visible the physicality of the act of speaking, as the speaker intentionally encounters his/her body as an instrument of communication.

Bourdieu posits that we incorporate the structure of cultural practice into our bodies, through which such structure becomes "natural."[30] Years prior to moving to the United States, I began incorporating the structure of normative communicative embodiment of SAE. Devika Chawla and Amardo Rodriquez provide a postcolonial critique of public speaking courses in which variously marginalized bodies (and tongues) are disciplined and regulated into normative acts of Western oral competency. They claim that since colonized bodies are physically and discursively regulated by others, we must attend to meanings assigned to these bodies and the normative behaviors that control them.[31] Learning how to speak SAE entailed regulating and disciplining my body into culturally and racially codified acts of oral competency. In this sense, my experience of racialization—or seeing my own body as evidence of otherness—is rooted not only in my visibly Asian body but more materially in the embodied struggle with habituating my body to speak in certain ways. The illusive normativity of whiteness becomes reified in relation to my unruly body that cannot quite conform to "proper" ways of speaking.

It was not just my tongue that I had to train to become a "fluent" English speaker. I had to retrain my ears. Again, in my English classes, my teacher would have us listen to audio recordings of native speakers of SAE and dictate the sentences for us to write down on a sheet of paper. Sitting at the desk with an audio player and skillfully pressing the buttons every few seconds, we would play and rewind the cassette tapes, patiently listening to the voice of the narrator through our headsets. I was determined to hear the unintelligible noise as articulate, linguistic sounds. Before I learned how to "listen" to English, I had to learn how to "hear" certain sounds as vocalized utterances with meaningful intention. As a student, I had to learn how to recognize certain sounds as meaningful sounds. It was a process through which a mysterious soundscape of SAE became a familiar acoustic environment of meaning, knowledge, and understanding. It is important to remember this act of hearing English is not an ideologically neutral process. I cultivated my ears specifically to listen to SAE, to recognize the sounds of voice uttered by educated US Americans as "proper" and "intelligible," to the extent that I would start hearing "accented" (or non-US) English as "different" and "unintelligible." In the hegemonic context of English as a global language, racial hierarchy is coded in this subtle yet problematic linguistic distinction of what is audibly intelligible and unintelligible—what the body can or cannot do matters especially in constituting cultural hegemony.[32] Thus, to give credence to whiteness in US contexts, I must first learn to recognize and "hear" its particular linguistic sounds as a source of legitimacy and credibility.

Even after a decade of studying and working in the United States, I still experience a sense of awe when I realize that I can "hear" and understand every English word uttered by someone, despite the fact that the English language still sounds foreign and alien to me. Speaking English as a second language means living with the seemingly bizarre auditory experience of a sense of disconnect between what I intend to say (meaning) and how it comes out (sound). It is a peculiar acoustic space in which I hear my voice saying the words that are supposed to convey what I intend to say, but I can never be absolutely certain about the accuracy of the sounds and pronunciations that come out of my mouth. The sounds that are specific to the English language do not belong to my vocal system; it is always a form of secondary imitation and approximation in which I orchestrate my vocal system to piece together the words and produce appropriate sounds. The dissonance I experience with the coordinated movement of my mouth, the sound of my utterance, and the supposed meaning I convey is fundamental to my experience of being a racial Other in the United States. The sense of racial alienation emerges from the sound of my voice that sounds foreign to my own ears in the racialized acoustic space of normative white speech.

After having lived in the United States for over five years, I visited my hometown and saw a friend from high school. Having a conversation in Japanese at a restaurant, he pointed out that my breathing is "Americanized"—a comment that simultaneously struck me and puzzled me. He explained that I used a deep abdominal breathing when I spoke and used a deeper voice, an observation that made me realize my breathing is more controlled when I speak English. I control my breathing so I can speak louder and more clearly, with a continuous flow of proper forms of enunciation and accent. I control my breathing to use a deeper voice because I want to convey authority and credibility, especially because of my raced and gendered identity as a woman of color in the United States. My habituated—albeit unconscious—ways of breathing while speaking English had seeped into my Japanese speech, which made my Japanese friend use the expression that my breathing is Americanized. Between the Japanese language and SAE, the rhythm of speech is different— that is, what "flows" in Japanese and English is different. So when I switch from one language to the other, I am not simply shifting my language; I am also shifting my bodily rhythm of how to punctuate my speech and control my breathing according to the conventional rhythm of the linguistic practice. When I speak Japanese, I speak more slowly, pacing myself with the nods and "uh huhs" of my interlocutor, sprinkling silence in between. When speaking Japanese, the codes of feminine gender performance must be embodied in my tone of voice, rhythm of speech, and bodily comportment. When I speak English, I attempt to defy the stereotypes of racialized and sexualized Asian femininity as soft-spoken, quiet, and submissive. I breathe in to verbalize my thoughts, to assert myself, to make a statement. I stand up straight, projecting confidence and making solid eye contact. In my experience, the process of code-switching is deeply visceral and embodied, fully engaging my culturally habituated and racially coded body.

When it comes to the constitution of my gendered identity in linguistic performance, I am not simply constituting an *idea* of femininity/masculinity through my speech; rather, I am constituting my body itself, a body that "properly" performs and embodies femininity/masculinity in certain linguistic contexts. Sustaining and reproducing ideologies requires bodies that enact and conform to normative ideas and practices. While an ideology—of linguistic gender performance, for example—gets embodied through rhythm, vocal tone, bodily movement, or breathing, in the process of performing such ideology we craft and constitute our bodily ways of being. Because I speak English in ways that are almost the same, but not quite, as native speakers of SAE, my habituated embodiment becomes a contested site of ideological reproduction and reification. Hegemonic ideologies embedded in SAE solidify legitimacy not merely symbolically, but also in the material and visceral experience of what my body can(not) do. As a speaker of English as a second language, I live in the liminal space between the cultural structures of embodiment in SAE and my habituated body's (in)ability to conform to such structures.

While speaking English is a full-body activity for me, it is also about speaking against my body—or defying what my body represents and proving it wrong. Although my "Americanized" speech keeps away the Orientalist gaze that undermines my authority and credibility as an Asian woman in the United States, it is this process of speaking white that inherently racializes my identity. I recall an exchange at the airport customs checkpoint, during which an immigration officer with a foreign accent processed my entry into the United States. He was clearly an immigrant from Latin America, but he treated me as if I had a questionable motive in coming to the United States. His demeanor was authoritative and unfriendly. I responded to his questions—"What do you study in the United States? When do you expect to graduate?"—with my standard American speech. I spoke back to his demeanor not through words, but through my assimilated cultural performance. This was a heightened moment of US hegemony: we were both trying to prove our allegiance to the United States. The officer enforced his patriotic duty of protecting the US border, while I gained my legal entry by living up to the status of an educated, assimilated Asian model minority.[33] It was an ironic moment, a case of mimicry—we both played the power game according to the master's rule that ultimately Otherized us as racial minorities.

The Twisted Tongue: A Phenomenology of Speaking White-While-Black (Chris)

When I was a young college student, I spoke to my white female professor about anxieties I experienced while taking standardized tests. She immediately deduced my experiences had little to do with testing anxieties and more to do with the fact that I was "bi-dialectal." Knowing I would struggle to maneuver my tongue to pronounce the syllables of this word, I asked, "What does *that* mean?" She responded, "Many African Americans are bi-dialectal, which means they have the ability to write and speak in two dialects." Obviously confused, I asked, "What does this have to do with my standardized test-taking abilities?" She responded, "Many educators believe that African Americans score low on aptitude tests because these tests reflect neither their commonly-held cultural experiences nor syntax." I found it difficult to understand how my cultural upbringing influenced my performance on standardized tests. So I asked, "Are you saying that because I don't speak *good* that I can't pass a test?" She replied, "No! Are you familiar with the term *Ebonics*?" I responded, "Yes, it's a derogatory term used to describe African American ways of speaking." She then said, "Not entirely! Black English Vernacular [BEV] is a creolized version of English based on a pidgin spoken by African slaves who struggled to make sense of the language of their captors." I was still somewhat confused, so she recommended that I read the works of Geneva Smitherman, Henry Louis Gates, and other scholars who see BEV as having a unique structural lexicon that is prominent in black speech patterns. Upon reading these works, I thought deeply about how I maintained a visceral allegiance to BEV while working to develop speech patterns of white SAE.

The phenomenon of *speaking white-while-black* enables an understanding of how the politics of race shape the embodied act of speaking, as exemplified in code-switching and styleshifting by black Americans.[34] This idea is useful to understand how many black Americans engage race-conscious speaking performances in cross-racial encounters. I recall struggling to manage the contradictory impulse to speak BEV around people of my race and to discipline my body to speak SAE around those who were racially different. However, this embodied linguistic flexibility developed as I moved out of my own cultural linguistic environments and into white social circles. As I moved within these spaces, I became mindful of the physical labor of using my throat, tongue, and lips while alternating between BEV and SAE. I also noticed that regardless of attempts to code-switch and styleshift, I still carried a "blaccent,"[35] producing sounds that follow from the styles, cadences, and rhythms rooted in black oral and rhetorical traditions. Nonetheless, speaking white-while-black highlights how racialized encounters dictate the physical act of speaking, illuminating my own bi-dialectal embodiment and the persisting racial ideologies inherent in our symbolic and linguistic systems of racialized interpersonal interactions.

As an undergraduate student, I started to understand how the act of speaking was loaded with racial identifications. While interacting with individuals from other racial groups who haphazardly mimicked black speech, I noticed they often omitted the "G" in words ending in "ing," emphasized the habitual "be" (e.g., he be trippin'), or emphatically stated multiple "yo's," or "whatz up witu's" while pointing their fingers and crossing their arms. Others spoke with an exaggerated form of slave speech, often starting with phrases like "y'all better," or "I'se a-gonna." Some have mimicked or corrected my own pronunciation as I used words such as "gotta," "nah," "wanna," "we be," "brotha" or "ax'em." To a great measure, their inability to enact or even embody the complexity of syntax and sound in black voice—including tone, inflection, and *soul*—was most revealing.[36] However, I not only learned that BEV is a not-so-distant cousin to what these individuals perceived as normalized SAE but also saw that BEV is more layered than just its unique syntax and sound. BEV maintains microlinguistic patterns combining elements of rhythm, resonance, phonation, vocal quality, and pitch that could not be easily duplicated.

As a graduate student and professor, I observed how my voice determined whether or not I was part of the ingroup, emphasizing membership within the black community, or outgroup wherein using SAE constitutes distancing oneself from black culture. In this way, voice became a signifier for power and privilege as I observed the policing of black bodies goes hand-in-hand with the policing of black voice. I found it quite ironic that some white and black educated elites, who embraced African American writers like Gwendolyn Brooks, Maya Angelou, and Alice Walker, were most resistant to firsthand performances of black language and styles symbolized in the work of these writers. For example, after giving a presentation on race relations, I was once advised to be much "quieter and gentler" (using minimal hand gestures and more subtle eye contact) when speaking to audiences of white professors to avoid being perceived as too preachy. Using black idiom is unprofessional in academia—highlighting not only outgroup members' discomfort with African American prose but also the troublesome insistence of the part of some to require black folks to change the way they speak to gain acceptance. Despite the fact that my black voice was often mocked and muted, and at times even admired, in the presence of those who are racially different, it underscores the paradox of the act of speaking that is both inclusive and exclusive.

The politics of speaking white-while-black highlights the racialized meanings within the embodied act of speaking. The process of embodying different speaking selves requires an engagement with the inner human experience, shaping both the internal acts (e.g., the intrinsic muscles allowing for the movement of the tongue) and external events (e.g., the interactions dictating speech and voice). At the most basic level, this embodied act of speaking is a product of my own-race and cross-race encounters as I physically alter my black voice to fit the contours of "proper" or "standard" English within white social spaces. As Sachi cautions, disciplining the body to speak white SAE is part of the process of cultural identity negotiation within the confines of dominant white cultural norms. At another level, the embodied act of code-switching is idiosyncratic, as sounds travel from the throat and through the mouth in coordination with unique ways of breathing, phonation, and resonance, depending on the interactants. Through experiences of moving within and among different racialized vantage points, I use a plurality of voices inscribed in different systems of expression—intonation, rhythm, and emphasis—and syntax and vocabulary.

Merleau-Ponty's claim that "it is the body which speaks"[37] does not refer to the fact that speaking depends upon airflow from the lungs making vocal chords in the larynx vibrate to create the vocal sound. Rather, the body is an expressive and intentional source of meaning. For Merleau-Ponty, the act of "speaking speech" (as opposed to "spoken speech"—expressions that transfer preexisting thoughts) has a signifying intention "at the stage of coming into being,"[38] which is to say that "speech itself *brings about* that concordance between me and myself, and between myself and others."[39] In these own-race and cross-race encounters, I was acutely aware of the differences in tone, pitch, sound, and even rhythm of BEV and SAE speakers. When engaging in own-race encounters, my black tongue easily strings together phrases and lines, including simile and metaphor in coordination with inflection and intonation, whereas in cross-race encounters, I must monitor my physical body, including my mouth and the sounds of my utterances. But, as Frantz Fanon suggests, racism unsettles the equilibrium of one's body, altering one's own tactile and visual experiences within a structure imposing "the 'racial parameters' within which the corporeal schema is supposed to fit."[40] For example, in cross-race encounters in which racial differences are readily apparent, internal and external energies that I am immediately aware of, and subjectively involved with, cause excess tension within the muscles of my larynx and muddle my tongue. To alleviate this tension, before speaking, I must engage in relaxed breathing, allowing enough air to my lungs and speaking with a lower pitch and slower speech rate to enhance vocal quality.

When I speak BEV, I know that I can easily say words like "walkin'," "talkin'," or "sleepin'" by gently placing my tongue against the hard palate of my mouth and simultaneously opening my mouth while relaxing my tongue in the lower jaw area. But when I try to speak SAE, the act of adding the "G" ending of these words requires taking short, quick breaths before engaging in the physical labor of thinking about how wide to open my mouth and where to place my tongue. This embodied act of speaking requires that I abruptly place my tongue against the hard palate of my mouth, and all at once, slightly push my tongue in between my lower and upper teeth while pushing my lips forward. Then, with my mouth remaining open, I tighten my jaws and pronounce the "G" sound and ending. My conscious engagement with these movements derived from admonishments from other white professors who have informed me that I must open my mouth wider when speaking SAE to say words such as "them" or "they" rather than "dem" or "dey"; there was also a professor who chided me for inaccurately saying "ax" rather than "ask" while teaching in the classroom—to which I took offense.

Speaking SAE has been as much about gaining flexibility in my tongue and jaws as it has been about pushing the limits of my vocabulary. Like Sachi, I too struggled to pronounce the "R" sound. Because most words in BEV require opening my mouth narrowly, I found it difficult to decipher how wide to open my mouth and where to place my tongue. As a result, when I pronounced the "R" sound, the sound came out as "Rra." So I practiced the act of simultaneously opening my mouth wide, relaxing my tongue, and sticking out my lips to produce the "R" sound of SAE. To this day, I feel uncomfortable when I eliminate the intensified continuative in a phrase like "he *steady* trippin'," or focus on adding the copula in phrases like "we cool." To be sure, when I say "he's overreacting" in the former, and "we're cool" in the latter, I feel like I am speaking with a voice that distances me—both bodily and culturally—from my racial group.

When code-switching from BEV to SAE, my sense of experience with rhythm, with respect to time, functions as an essence of my own-race and cross-race encounters. Rhythm is pre-reflexive and pre-verbal as it manifests in our bodies while interacting with others in our everyday lives. When speaking BEV with the members of my own racial group, I experience the rhythm of speaking that emerges in us and between us within the conversational flow, activating a shared use of syntax, variation of vocal pitch—higher, faster, and slower, and elongation signaling intonation—variations in loudness—signaling emotion—and even more tactical rhetorical strategies, including repetition (repeating words or statements) and call and response. The spontaneous reciprocity and exchange of rhythm become a performance of our own making, as they are already present within our common cultural experiences. Then again, cross-race encounters, at times, interfere with personal experiences of rhythm. When speaking SAE, it takes time for me to find and feel the rhythm of speaking. I often lose my sense of rhythm while speaking, as I experience struggles with breathing—affecting vocal speed and pitch—to engage pauses in turn-taking, and to coordinate what I desire to say with what actually comes out (sound), impacting vocal quality. In cross-race encounters, rhythm is anticipatory, emerging in the process of sensing and being sensed,[41] as my voice takes on the rhythm mirroring those with power who influence my existence. It is another ironic case of mimicry—regardless of how much I appreciate and enjoy expressing metaphors, the habitual "be," and simile spoken in BEV, and experimenting with new sayings using the tongue. As an educated black man, I am largely measured by how closely I mimic and conform to dominant white speaking norms. While it is no secret that many whites and even some blacks view BEV through the racially charged lens of intellectual inferiority, understanding the materially felt labor of speaking becomes yet another way to appreciate how black voice gives resonance to the narratives of struggle of black people.[42]

Conclusion: The Politics of Habituated Embodiment

We began with a simple yet often unexamined question: How do we emerge as embodied communicative subjects through the act of speaking? Speaking is an act of being and becoming; we invariably become the language we speak. Speech acts contour the body not only as a surface on which cultural inscriptions take place but more fundamentally as a living, sensuous organism that is actively and proactively open to the social and material world. In Sachi's narrative, learning how to speak SAE was an embodied process of acquiring new types of bodily and sensory experiences, deeply intertwined with cultural and ideological structures of the dominant US culture. In Chris's account of speaking white-while-black, learning how to speak SAE was an embodied process of code-switching between his BEV and SAE voices.

What we want to highlight is the following idea: it is not just what we say—although we can never separate what and how—but how we say it and which racial and cultural ideologies are sedimented and habituated in our lived bodies. For example, the ideologies of whiteness ingrained in the sound of SAE materialize in Sachi's habituated act of "hearing" SAE speech as a legitimate, credible, and normative linguistic sound. In Chris's experience, he is urged to code-switch and styleshift at the level of bodily enactment and modification— from rolling the tongue and opening the mouth wider, to altering the rhythm of his speech—in order to perform a "legitimate" academic identity. Underneath our symbolic expressions within the conceptual and ideological universe of language, the act of speaking requires a body that speaks, hears, and moves in accordance with the given cultural and ideological habitus.

At the most basic level, the phenomenology of speaking points to the fact that symbolic activities require a material body that does things—an idea seemingly obvious yet under-theorized. The anatomy of speaking bodies has been examined from the lens of linguistic science or neuropsychological explanations of communicative bodies that approach communication as a largely autonomous and subjectless function.[43] We examined the performative effects of the act of speaking on the formation of subjectivity by foregrounding habituated embodiment as a contested medium of symbolic activity and meaning-making. Our inquiry resonates with those who provide materialist analyses on the impact of technological infrastructures and material arrangements on communication.[44] Instead of looking at the body as a technology, however, we believe the communicative body is a sensuous, sensible, and sense-making entity that contours and is contoured by bodily experiences. Thus, if Butler's discussion on performativity pointed to the poststructuralist understanding of how bodies come to matter through citational discourse, then our inquiry highlights the body as always-already more than discursive.[45] Meaning gets sedimented not in what is said (signifier), but in the material process of accomplishing the signifier (the materialization of a speaking body as a medium of communication). Communication is a contested process of becoming an embodied communicative body, one that can(not) do things "properly" in a given context.

The speaking body is a medium of reproducing a hegemonic habitus, a social environment in which a particular "mode of dramatizing or enacting possibilities" is legitimated over others.[46] At the same time, the speaking body is a disciplinary device to remember and reproduce the bodily ways of being we inherit from our culture. Our "failure" to conform to the normative speech patterns of SAE reveals that while a "signifying act delimits and contours the body," the body is not passively awaiting its signification and contouring by hegemonic discourses.[47] Rather, it is through enactive bodily participation in the act of speaking that we emerge as embodied speaking subjects. Despite our embodied efforts to conform to or mimic SAE, our always-already habituated bodies fail us in becoming normative speakers of SAE. The limits of social construction are not merely discursively defined; rather, the limits of normativity/Otherness are experientially reified through what a habituated body can or cannot do "properly." The politics of a normative communicative body is not just a matter of ideological signification but also about what kind of habituated lived embodiments or bodily-ways-of-being-in-the-world are allowed to exist physically and materially. The path toward counter-hegemonic ways of being begins, at least partially, with our critical and reflexive awareness of direct bodily experiences within larger material and ideological contexts.

We attempted to make a methodological intervention in critical qualitative research by returning to the direct bodily experience that may slip through more conventional symbolic naming and ideological analysis. We contend that critical qualitative research benefits from attending to more implicit and material grounding of cultural hegemony and ideological contouring. In this sense, we situate our lived bodies as always-already mindful and sensuous; we "think" in and through our enactive-bodies-in-context, rather than merely in our heads. In our phenomenological descriptions, we purposefully and intentionally decentered the rational and logical "I," and foregrounded the mindful and sensuous body as a lived instrument of the politics of communication. Our social and ideological experiences are materially and bodily grounded, making the body a contested site, not only of symbolic representations but also of material manifestations and embodiments of power.

The path toward a more sensorially materialist understanding of embodiment in communication, then, is to (re)locate the nuanced politics of performativity in the phenomenological materiality of the sensuous body without collapsing the lived body into either biology or discursive conditions and ideological structures. Our inquiry into the act of speaking illuminates the phenomenological materiality of the body and embodiment inherent in our symbolic, linguistic, and discursive activities as communicators. Our narratives demonstrate how the cultural and ideological aspect of speaking intertwines with the physical, material, and bodily dimensions of speaking.[48] Our thick descriptions of direct bodily experiences illuminate how dominant ideologies deploy and recruit our bodies-in-action, and how acts of assimilation and resistance are materially enacted and nuanced. While the visibility of cultural inscription on the body-as-surface is always a valuable source of deconstructive critique, scholars must also attend to the discursively invisible, yet materially felt labor of bodies that speak.

6

Sensing Empathy in Cross-Racial Interactions

The clock was ticking as I, Chris, had only a few weeks to find and interview white men in leadership positions within their organization for a research project focusing on their views on leadership and diversity. For my last set of interviews, I returned home to Chicago, Illinois. There was not much time left, so as soon as I arrived on the airplane from Albuquerque, New Mexico, I immediately got on a train and headed toward downtown Chicago. When I walked out of the train station, I felt the warm breeze from Lake Michigan touch my face, and saw the tall buildings situated in a row along the Magnificent Mile, an exclusive section on Michigan Avenue. The buildings were quite familiar but I was somehow disoriented. I somehow lost my bearings! *What street should I turn onto from Michigan Avenue? How does the building where I will conduct the interview look? Oh my, I hope I am not late for my appointment. I've been in this very spot hundreds of times; how and why am I lost?* I turned onto a street off of Michigan Avenue, hoping to reorient myself. As I started walking in between the skyscrapers, I felt a strong gust of wind hit my face so I closed my eyes and tucked my chin toward my chest. I didn't want to create the impression that I was lost so I walked hurriedly with a swarm of people who were either running to catch a bus or rushing to find a place to eat lunch. I moved my arms and legs in the same pace, tempo, and rhythm of the horde—a way of fitting in with, and feeling like, other Chicagoans.

As I walked with the crowd, this tingling feeling in my stomach alerted me to the fact that I was moving further away from my destination. So, I stopped and slightly turned to look around. The passersby walking behind me swiftly swerved around me as I stood still. A couple of people slightly bumped me as they held their heads down to cover their faces from the gust of wind. I finally located an empty space near the revolving door of a building and quickly dodged the passersby to get there. When I arrived near the side of the revolving door—away from the hustle and bustle of the afternoon rush—I stood and thought: *Where is this damn building?* I had neither a cell phone nor a map. I hoped that my own instincts would lead the way, or that I could recognize something familiar. Since I was still lost, I thought it would be best to ask for help. Out of the corner of my eye, I saw a white woman approaching the building. As she moved closer to the revolving door, I made eye contact with her and asked, "Excuse me, could you . . . " but she walked through the revolving door, ignoring me as if I were standing erect like a mere statue. She either thought I was a panhandler, or was scared of me, or both. But, I couldn't worry about it—I had to find the building. I didn't want to be too late.

Much of the crowd went by so I stepped away from the building while mentally mapping the streets of downtown Chicago. *Alright, the lake is to the East; that means that this way* (turning to my body to the North) *is toward Navy Pier and the Water Tower. Okay, this way* (turning my body to the South) *is toward Solider Field; this way is toward the United Center* (turning my body to the West). I started walking west—*this is the direction that I needed to go.* As I walked westward, I started recalling the street names and numbers, and the location of certain buildings. I regained my sense of direction and eventually found the place where I would conduct my first interview of the afternoon. Once I found the building, I entered the revolving doors and got on the elevator. The elevator ascended and reached its stopping point—*ding*! I walked onto a floor where I saw an office with two glass double doors, and where a receptionist was seated behind a counter. At other interviews, my interactions with the receptionists and office assistants, all white and female, were cordial but some paused before speaking to me while others asked questions as if they were suspicious of my meeting with their employer. It didn't matter that I was wearing a shirt, tie, and slacks. I was young, black, and male—in all likelihood, I didn't fit the profile of people who usually come to their office. I walked into the office and in the direction of the counter. To my surprise, there was a black woman seated behind the counter. I mused, *wow, cool, I finally get to meet a black person.* She was not only the first black receptionist but the only black person that I encountered during my visits to the offices of these white male leaders. She was talking on the telephone so I moved to an empty seat nearby. We made eye contact. She, too, looked quite surprised as she removed her mouth from the telephone receiver, and stated, "One moment." I felt a sense of calm—a profound sense that I was in the presence of someone who looked like me.

I suspected that she would be neither confused nor leery of my scheduled appointment. So, when she hung up the telephone, I confidently walked toward the counter and said, "Hello, I have an appointment with Steve." She looked into my eyes with a sharp stare, and shook her head from side-to-side. She seemed incredulous and said, "Yeah right, alright quit playing around! Why are you here?" I stood back from the counter ever so slightly and slowly—I felt my bottom lip stiffen and eyes squint as I peered into her eyes in disbelief. I quickly bit my bottom lip and then rubbed them together before saying, "I have a scheduled meeting with Mr. Steve Johnson. Please call his assistant and tell her that Christopher is here." Obviously befuddled, she asserted, "Sir, if you don't tell me why you are here, I am going to call the building security. So, again, tell me why you are here?" I stood with my hands on my hips for a few seconds, as we stared into each other's eyes refusing to yield. She repeated, "If you aren't going to tell me why you are here, then you will have to leave." There was an overwhelming intensity as she was leery of my presence. I presumed that it was indeed rare for a black person to come into contact with anyone in this office or that she embraced some internalized racist propaganda, reinforcing negative stereotypes about black male underachievement—after all, why would someone like me have a meeting with the chief executive officer of her company? After some silence, I replied, "I don't understand why you cannot just call his Assistant? She will clear everything up." She picked up the phone and said, "I'm calling security." I stood now with my arms folded across my chest, thinking *here we go again*. Suddenly, I heard someone's voice, presumably Steve's assistant, off in the distance, "Is Steve's ten o'clock appointment here?" Because it was late, she came to see if I had arrived. The receptionist quickly looked in my direction and then at Steve's assistant. His assistant suddenly appeared around the corner and spotted me. She stated, "Oh Christopher, right?" I replied, "Yes, I am here to meet with Mr. Johnson." She responded, "Come to the back, follow me. Did you have a hard time finding the building?" I replied, "Yes, I got lost but I eventually found it." After meeting with Steve, I walked toward the front desk to leave. The receptionist and I made eye contact. Needless to say, it was of the unfriendly kind but I refrained from fretting over it. As we looked at each other, I stopped near the counter and said, "I get it. Okay, it's all good. Have a nice day, sista!" As I continued toward the door, she smirked and slowly nodded her head up and down.

In situations where I have met or walked past black people in spaces where mostly white people walk, talk, and meet, I have been always comforted with the kind of mutual recognition and solidarity either through a head nod or through verbal acknowledgments of "hello" or "*wuz up*." So, I struggled with the lack of mutual acknowledgment between us. I struggled with feeling through her gaze (reinforcing suspicions of the black male body) and my own bodily posture standing with my arms crossed (reinforcing the black masculine trope that inducts gender into the fold via a brief indulgence with strength), that our sense of blackness was curbed by the sleek office space where mostly white people conduct business—a space where neither someone like me is likely to inhabit, nor someone like her is likely to work. More precisely, I struggled with the lack of kinesthetic empathy between us, involving the absence of intersubjective rhythms and understandings of race mediated by mutual feelings of bodily alienation and isolation in predominantly white spaces.[1]

Feeling Empathy in Intersubjective Encounters

Intersubjective encounters can produce changes in our embodied experiences where we unexpectedly feel the sensorimotor and emotional responses of empathy across, between, and through bodies in interaction. The sensory input and output along with emotions of happiness, anger, and sadness transmitted body-to-body can produce intense feelings, triggering reflections on the world we live in. The literature on empathy is quite extensive in psychiatry, psychotherapy, and philosophy.[2] For instance, Edith Stein posits that empathy involves the condition through which one is subjected to the experiences of another, as the *Other*.[3] Stein asserts that individuals develop empathy through a process of viewing the emergence of the Other's experience, situating oneself in the place of the Other, and by providing a comprehensive account of the Other's experience.[4] Carl Rogers uses the term "empathy" to discuss a counseling technique for reflecting back on the meaning of what clients appear to say rather than simply repeating their words.[5] Peter Breggin theorizes that counselors who reflect on their own emotions will develop the capacity to create empathy for their clients' concerns.[6] Importantly, empathy as a phenomenon is unlike forms of sympathy. Sympathy as a phenomenon of communication involves commiserating or *feeling for* the other's affliction; whereas, empathy develops from a *feeling into*, a "motor mimicry" or "inner imitation" applied to knowing the other's feelings.[7] Although Stein describes empathy as an encounter with a "foreign" consciousness—"the experience which an 'I' as such has another 'I' as such."[8] She explains that such an experience is not so much with having the other's experience, but having preexisting experiences that trigger the foreignness of the "I." As Maurice Merleau-Ponty once stated, "It is as if the other person's intention inhabited my body."[9] Although not always explicated in research on race and whiteness, the examination of how intersubjective experiences of race challenge, transact, and even transform everyday systems of racial inequities has been important in anti-racist thought. In the following, I explore the possibility of cross-racial empathy, producing felt rhythms and a visceral *feeling-with* in cross-racial interactions. Empathetic connections get established as bodies interact and entrain themselves into the rhythm, tempo, and sensations of one another's lived experience.

In this chapter, I reflect on how the bodily sensorial experiences called forth feelings, or lack thereof, of empathy with the white male elites I interviewed for my project.[10] Mind you, I am an African American male interviewer interested in understanding their perspectives on topics of leadership and diversity.[11] Scholars of race have often neglected the expressions of white male elites.[12] Instead, they analyzed the discourses of ordinary white people such as college students.[13] Previous studies have shown that many white people intentionally steer clear of conversations on race with people of color.[14] While it is rare for whites to talk about discernible, tacit knowledge of racism, most of these men openly shared their racial stories with me.[15] For instance, one man told a story of an encounter with civil rights marchers in the 1960s; another man shared a story about working with people from different cultural backgrounds while in the Peace Corps; others shared stories on watching their children play with other children of color; and being reared to be colorblind. Whereas most repeated the oft-recited progressive narratives of valuing difference in their stories, two men, of whom I will call Greg, a CEO of an organization, and Stuart, a US attorney, talked about their struggles with being targets of racism. The following is designed to walk the reader through these experiences with the knowledge that racial understandings vary across and within racial groups.[16] I provide descriptions of these two white male elite's stories by highlighting, first, their experiences of racism in a real-life drama that produced powerful feelings that involved me as a witness to, and eventually a participant in, the retelling of their stories. Second, I write about the senses of cross-racial empathy, shaping how we feel and come to think about race and racism. I treat empathy as embodied, as involving our shared, felt sensory modalities that are mediated intersubjectively and yet fraught with discord.

"Racism 101"

One day, I interviewed Greg in an office building in downtown Chicago. Greg spoke extensively on an array of ideas involving leadership and the culture of his organizations. Truth be told, we both shared our ideas on these topics as he was interested in my perspective. After the interview, Greg was grateful for the opportunity to talk openly about ideas that were already percolating at some subconscious level, but it was a question on diversity training programs that compelled him to talk about an experience of struggling with racism.

To set the scene of my interviews, knowing that the term "diversity" often times enters the workplace as a form of public relations and as a directive from management, I asked these white men to talk about how they convince their employees that diversity training is in the best interest of the company. Since most of these men required their employees to attend yearly diversity training programs, I asked them to talk about its effectiveness. Some believed that forced compliance hindered its effectiveness, while others believed that these programs lacked any real influence on the bottom line. Similarly, Greg discussed a few of the important steps that he implemented to improve diversity training, but he lamented the antipathy it often created in his employees. In following up, I asked Greg to talk about the cause of the general animus felt by his employees. As he sat in silence while pondering my question, the absence of noise in the room made me feel uneasy. So, I quickly rubbed my beard with the tips of my thumb and index fingers to create my own scratchy sound. I started to wonder if the question was unbefitting, but I waited, foreswearing the impulse to ask a question on a different topic. Greg stared in my eyes while nodding slowly up and down. He then leaned back in his chair, tapped his index finger on the desk, and finally just said, "Alright, let's see" and paused once again. I put down my formal interview script as I gathered that he had something much deeper and more profound to say. Even as Greg's body remained stationary in the chair, I felt the tension grow with every strike of his finger on the desk. I focused on the sensations within the moment including how I felt the strength of his silence and eye contact. This process of sensing and making sense involved enduring in silence with Greg while having the felt sense of hearing, seeing, and touching of objects around us. Finally, Greg said, "You know, diversity trainings should include stories like this!"

About five years before this interview, Greg and his wife, who I will call, Diana, adopted a "very dark-skinned" one-year-old girl from India who I will call Bahula. One day, they were in the grocery store. As Bahula sat in the grocery cart, a "kindly looking" elderly white woman walked toward her. The woman's eyes touched the skin of Bahula's face and then stared, confusingly, at Greg and Diana. As Greg and Diana smiled with hopes of sharing their excitement with her, the befuddled lady stated, "Is this your daughter?" Greg replied, "Why yes, we just adopted her!" The elderly women then murmured, "Oh my, she is so dark. How could you kiss her?" As Greg and Diana stood shocked (with their hands over their wide-opened mouths) and florid, the elderly woman abruptly walked toward the checkout counter.

After telling this story, Greg at once slapped the palm of his hand on the top of the desk and shouted, "Bam!" I felt the vibration from the slapping noise of his hand coming in contact with the desk. Feeling the sound effect of the word "bam" and the tactility of the slapping noise in my inner ear sparked my own frustrations with feeling overwhelmingly isolated or powerless in the face of discrimination. Like someone without a friend; like someone feeling the strain of the other's intolerance to the limit. Across these sensations, I started to hear and see Greg unravel and share emotions of anger and withdrawal associated with the victimization of his dark-skinned daughter. As a black man, I found myself sympathizing with him as I *felt into* his story. As he continued,

> Welcome to racism 101! When you get those rose colored glasses shattered.
> [*He pauses*] There are some racist people out there. You want to shield your
> daughter from situations at playgrounds where a mother picks up her kids
> from playing with her, and [places] them with some white kids.

Greg and I sat silently for a few seconds. Sitting in silence became part of the rhythm of this intersubjective encounter, allowing us to think through and feel the disgust and anger that he and Diana experienced. The experience of witnessing the elderly white woman's racist labeling of his adopted daughter as "too dark" to deserve affection through the characterization of "racism 101" underscored not only Greg's introduction to the traumatic feelings of being subjected to blatant racism but also the sense of feeling like an outsider within the perceptibly safe white space of his neighborhood grocery store. Greg's use of the phrase "racism 101" acted as a sensor, enabling me to reexperience bodily reactions that I felt as a target of racist epithets and acts. As Walter Benjamin puts it, storytellers are embodied both as the speaking subject and as the subject of discourse; they also are part of an intersubjective system where the audience (in this case, the interviewer) is drawn to share the language and emotion of the experience itself.[17] His experience thus was accessible to me; I felt sympathy internally in my body—a feeling that I rarely, if ever, have felt with another white person while talking about racism. As he spoke, I shared nods of agreement, feeling simultaneously impulses of distress and compassion as he imagined what life may be like for Bahula, as the only girl of color on the playground where white kids play.

Still, I felt uncomfortably distanced from his physical white body, leery of the fact that even in chaos, whiteness reworks and rehabilitates itself.[18] As a black man, who, like many African Americans, endured "racism 101" moments early in life, I found it difficult to reconcile his experience in the grocery store with the racially hegemonic position that grants him social and material privileges.[19] Indeed, Greg felt the shock as his mouth was left wide open in hearing the woman's racist animus of his white lips touching the dark skin of his infant daughter. But perhaps, my evolving empathetic physiological responses derived not from Greg's own deeply visceral experiences of his "racism 101" moment, but from thinking about how Bahula will experience the racial sensorium as she comes to know and experience the world.

Nonetheless, I explored possibilities for deeper feelings of empathy so I momentarily departed from my preoccupation with the self, as the interviewer. I shared a story with Greg of a research project where I spent countless days and hours reading manifestos from leaders of online hate groups and listening to white racialist music. I briefly stated, "One day, I ventured onto a white supremacist online chat room and started to talk with its members in real time. After a brief exchange, a hacker kicked me out of the chat room by blackening my computer screen and electronically scripting a statement in red letters, resembling dripping blood: 'Get off this computer Nigger!'" I paused for a moment hoping to share in the same silence that I afforded him. But Greg immediately stated, "Wow, it had to be difficult to go on those websites."

I responded, "At first, yes, but not really"—signaling in fact that it was not the point of my story. I then explained briefly, "We can no longer understand diversity just through artificial categories of difference without considering how encounters like yours and *mine* are part of the tensions of a white supremacist system." Greg nodded in agreement. I was certainly surprised with this gesture of affirmation, so I asked him, "How do we develop diversity training programs with content that reveals these tensions captured in racist interactions like the one you and Diana, and I experienced?" He replied, "I don't think it is necessary to go that far," [*he pauses*] raising his hand with this palm facing me—parallel to my chest. I slumped my shoulders in seeing his palm in front me—a felt physiological response that physically stopped me. As he spoke, my eyes detached from his eyes moving toward the skyscrapers outside of his office window. That sudden sense of curiosity and intrigue is now replaced with feelings of emptiness. As I peered outside of the window, I gathered my thoughts and reoriented my body in thinking maybe he viewed white supremacy as rooted solely in Neo-Nazi propaganda. I slowly exhaled through my nose while ever so slightly smirking, feeling that the possibility of empathy was somewhat compromised. He then asserted,

Look! My employees [mostly white] just need exposure. They come from background[s] where they have no experience with people like the KKK.

They live in [my neighborhood], where they raise "tolerant" (making air quotes with his fingers) kids. [*He pauses*] So, it is a good experience to see that sort of thing; to remind ourselves that these people exist in the world so that they don't forget that it could still happen.

Greg lamented that his employees and white people in his neighborhood require exposure to blatant forms of racism. Possibly, the series of pauses or my lack of eye contact prompted him to suspend ordinary feelings of white liberal tendency to disaffiliate from white supremacy in cross-racial dialogues.[20] Still, as my eyes met his eyes, I struggled to relocate any felt sense of engaging in an empathetic, intersubjective encounter. My body was awakened by strange sensations evinced in otherness and difference—a disruption in my venture to feel cross-racial empathy. I relented to the assumption that white people struggle, almost with a gut reaction of discomfort or defensiveness, to talk about racism especially when implicating their experiences in white supremacy.[21] I still was encouraged by the fact that we progressed to reimagining how our experiences, and those alike, could potentially add to understandings of race in diversity training programs. As Greg continued,

I think this is the kind of training that people should have. Not that we should get along stuff [*sic*]. Experiences like these are real wakeup calls. Most people that I come across are not blatantly racist, but they have tendencies to ascribe a behavior to one type of person, like holding their purse if you see a black man, kind of thing.

As I nodded my head, maintained eye contact, and leaned back into my chair, I felt a sense of calm in listening to Greg label his experience as a "real wakeup call" not only for him, but for other white people that he personally knows. He believes that racist stereotypes of African American men that cause a white woman to touch, feel, and grip her purse are real and necessary to be addressed in diversity training. The gesture of using his palm to steer away from my experience still resonates, however. I could not shrug off my own distrusting glances and uptight posture in feeling that the journey toward understanding structural racism persisted on his terms. I felt that the conversation was no longer ours; rather, I had to prioritize his white feelings as valid. I felt my body shutdown—biting my tongue, folding my hands together in front of my mouth while sitting quietly. I would rather the conversation fall short of deeper meanings of these experiences than to emotionally exhaust myself trying to talk about how white supremacy systematically affects racist interactions like his own. After some conversation on the lack of "real" racist experiences in diversity training workshops, Greg ended with the following short story:

> My daughter goes to this nice private school. There was an e-mail exchange where somebody said that their point was devalued, and someone else said we value everybody's point. The next thing you know, all us [sic] white upper-middle class, liberal parents are at a useless day-long seminar on diversity because of two people bitching [sic]. And those who needed it didn't show up.

Early on, I sensed that with their florid faces and wide-open mouths, Greg only vaguely knew and had never really felt what it was like to have someone they love become a target of racism. But, after being physically and emotionally jolted by the racist remarks of the elderly white woman, Greg developed a racial awareness stimulating potential changes in his company's diversity training program. Through initiating eye contact, shunning the discomfort of silence, and simply nodding my head, I not only felt empathy for his daughter but in some ways sympathy for Greg. He developed a racial self-consciousness in negotiating his own understandings of the psychological comforts and discomforts of seeing places, like the grocery store where his "rose-colored glasses [were] shattered," as race neutral. He learned, as a white co-parent of an adopted child of color, that race is really a meaningful symbol of difference wherein people of color must coordinate their actions and meanings to other white people.[22] He imagines that he must negotiate interactions in neutral spaces, like the playground, where he would have to "shield [his] daughter from [racist acts]" whose body is inscribed with racial meanings that are socially and historically constructed. He thus imagines how racism feels on her body.

Greg captured the evolving sense of his racial self, as an employer and a father, through an experience understood as his own "racism 101." Physically, Greg and I felt the intensity and emotions through our use of silence and pauses to reflect on particular layers of his story. Yet, I invariably teetered on the fringes of empathy. I felt leery as he used the pronoun "they" to distance himself from other whites (especially those who hold racist stereotypes against African American men, who lack experiences like his own, or who *need* to attend diversity training). I felt and sensed my own numbness, as invoking the pronoun "they" in regard to race makes white people see themselves as exceptions, or one of the few who are free from the liability of racism. I thus felt disruptions in cross-racial empathy within this interview as Greg reflected on his visceral experiences of racism, but disaffiliated from whiteness as a source of his own critical race awareness.

"Being Called a F***in' Kike"

I interviewed another man, Stuart, in his office in downtown Chicago. When I arrived at his office, I immediately recognized photos of famous athletes from a US city on the East Coast on the wall. So I asked, "Are you from [there]?" Stuart smiled and replied, "Oh yes, that is where I was born." I then asked, "Well, what was it like living [there]?" Stuart stated that he grew up in an "all-white middle-class neighborhood" with his father who was an attorney and mother who was a homemaker. I immediately considered how my blackness factored in his response when Stuart suddenly shifted from talking about his upbringing to his experiences of race while attending a private school in his neighborhood:

The school I went to was an Episcopalian school. It was a 200 year old church-affiliated school and I am Jewish. [*He laughs*] There were very few minorities; there were two African Americans and one Asian. I can't think of any Hispanics. I was one of the few Jews in my class, but we all could pass for white, well-off Protestants and Catholics too [*He laughs again*].

As he laughed, I chuckled immediately after. The physical, rhythmical sounds of our laughter seemed to lighten the burden of talking about race, diversity, and leadership. I sensed, as he held his smile long after the laughter ended, that he wanted to talk more deeply about issues of identity in his childhood. So I again placed my interview script aside, eschewing questions of diversity and race. Instead, I adapted questions to Stuart's responses on attending an Episcopalian school. Specifically, I was intrigued with his statement on *passing* in repressing his Jewish identity to maintain the privileges of being considered "white." Stuart's whiteness is a *disidentifier* permitting the concealment of his Jewish identity.[23] As he leaned back in his chair while smiling, I asked, "How did your perceived status as a white, Protestant or Catholic, male influence the degree to which you acknowledged your Jewish identity among your peers?" Stuart sighed, sat in silence, and rubbed his right hand against right cheek. I sat still as he carefully contemplated an answer. I appreciated the slow pace and care he took in pondering my question, as he said:

Okay, I felt a great deal of anti-Semitism at the school. I was called derogatory names. They tried to get under my skin. I also heard a lot of people say negative things about Jews and racial minorities when they didn't know I was Jewish.

Stuart stopped speaking, looked down at his desk, and fidgeted with a pen. I sensed that he wanted to say more, but struggled to find the appropriate words. In silence, I kept eye contact while slowly nodding my head. I sat with my chin resting in between my index finger and thumb. I then slowly rubbed the palm of my hand over my mouth. In this way, I felt and showed empathy for the dehumanizing experience of being the target of a derogatory comment. In fact, I *felt with* him and presupposed that I could imagine what he was thinking. So,

I asked if I could share a story about an altercation that I had with a white man while traveling in Mexico as a college student. Stuart obliged, so I explained:

One day I walked along a road without a sidewalk with a few friends. Earlier that week, I severely sprained my ankle so I limped with a cane that I borrowed from a friend on the trip. As we walked along the road, a car approached. My friends and I moved closer to the edge of the road to allow the car to go by. Since I limped slowly to the edge, a man, a middle-aged white guy, continuously honked his horn. I reached the edge along with my friends and he slowly drove past us, yelling "get outta of the way Nigger!" Surprised and shocked, I yelled and retorted, "what did you say, muthaf**ker?" The car stopped and the door opened. Out walked this tall white dude; he was about 7 inches taller and much heavier than me. The man quickly moved toward me. My friends were aghast, and some started to yell. I could not move, so I lifted the cane in the air, like a baseball player preparing to hit a ball, and balanced myself on one leg with my injured leg slightly in the air. He suddenly stopped, realizing that I was not going to limp away in fear. As he ran back to his car, I saw a white woman in the passenger seat yelling, "Get back in the car!" I watched in earnest as I thought he was going to grab some kind of weapon. But, he drove a short distance ahead to flag down the police. The police arrived at the scene and immediately came toward me with their fists balled up ready to fight as the man yelled, "Arrest the little black son of a bitch!" After the man drove away, the police stood in front me with their fists clenched—I didn't feel their anger or take heed to their threatening pose because I was so fixated on the white guy. All the while, my friend, who spoke fluent Spanish, explained haplessly what happened to one of the police officers. Since I could no longer see the man in the distance, my attention turned to the police where one officer stood in front of me, rolling up his sleeves. I could see the hate in his eyes, as he sized me up. I kept staring past him looking in the direction where the car disappeared—I wasn't concerned about the cop or that I was in a foreign country. I was still fuming from hearing the white guy call me both a "nigger" and "little black son of a bitch." Suddenly, the other police officer who was speaking with my friend turned to his partner and said something in Spanish. His partner nodded and backed away. The officer then asked us not to come around this area. As we walked away, my friend told us the police knew this man and he was a very important person in the area. She said that they had to follow his orders even if he was in the wrong.

I watched Stuart as he hung on every word of my story while keeping a strong steady gaze with frequent head nods. The immediacy of watching the affirming movements of his head, and watching his eyes touch my eye as if he tried to peer into my skull exhorted me to talk openly about strong feelings of anger that were aroused from hearing the racist epithet from the white man and observing the capitulation of the police. There seemed to be a synchrony involving the mutual alignment of our sensorial rhythms (be it through eye contact or nodding or shaking heads) around the felt impulses of my experience. As I sat in silence, Stuart stated, "Wow that really happened. You were pretty lucky, huh." I responded, "I am not sure that it is about luck, but I am sympathetic to the fact that derogatory statements can induce anger or confusion when . . ." Stuart immediately interrupted,

Right! But okay. I almost fought with a friend one time who said, when we were kind of joking about something, "You are such a Jew!" I said, "You know I am Jewish, don't you." He said, "What? You are Jewish? Man, I am sorry. I didn't mean to say that." I said, "Don't you understand that there is a problem here? You shouldn't be thinking like that, but if you do, don't say anything. You don't perpetuate these kinds of stereotypes by talking about a group of people like this, whether it is Jews, Blacks, Hispanics, [or] Asians." We weren't friends after that. So I was kind of a fish out of water to a large degree in that school. I identified more with and preferred to be with other minorities. I didn't like walking the halls of my prep school with just blond-haired and blue-eyed white kids.

While it appeared that my story prompted Stuart to talk about this occurrence with his friend, his use of the phrase "Right! But okay," as an interruption, produced a barrier between himself and me. As he interrupted, I stopped and slowly slumped in my chair. While he spoke, I listened but I felt like he wanted to participate in some kind of oppression Olympics, as if fighting his friend was paramount to hearing a strange white man use a racial epithet to refer to me, or even watching the police justify or pretend to heed his demands. Stuart evoked this response to fulfill some expectation of the self rather than being made co-present in acknowledging, taking up, and mirroring the experience of a body that is different from his own. In reflection, Greg, on the one hand, was genuinely shocked when hearing the racist comment from the elderly woman in using the metaphor of "racism 101" to highlight distressed feelings of the initial encounter with racism. Stuart, on the other hand, appeared largely displaced and unsettled in a segregated prep school where racist statements were shared among those who were white. Stuart overheard racist comments from his peers who were unaware of his Jewish identity, but he resisted only when his own whiteness was challenged by a white friend who playfully referred to him as a "Jew." So, I wanted to hear more. I rephrased my question, "How did you feel about passing as a white student while being privy to conversations that were blatantly racist?" Stuart continued,

Honestly, I don't know. I was brought up to be proud of my faith and traditions. Despite being called a fuckin' kike to my face, I never lost pride in my people. But, I was torn between fighting and turning the other cheek. Both of my parents wanted me to go in there and kick some people's asses. I did once or twice, but I hated myself for doing it. I was forced to be violent and defend myself physically. I felt persecuted, hated, marginalized, humiliated, [and] belittled. It made me feel even worse that I was reduced to physical violence to salvage my pride. I hated it! [I tried other things], but I just found that a bigot is a bigot. [They were] brought up to hate others, and I'm sure they are the same people now.

Admittedly, I felt the tentative nature of my own cross-racial empathy, pondering the felt experience of the incoherence between having a racially privileged body while being alienated from those who, too, are racially privileged. Stuart was able to associate but challenge whites who made racist comments, but also was the target of white derogatory ascriptions prompting some felt sense of identification with minorities in his prep school. Although this is a case of whiteness securely orienting itself in all interracial spaces,[24] I sensed a layer of empathy in the kind of negotiation of rivaling emotional subjectivities and kinesthetic comportment that I often experience in interracial interactions. The deepening pathos of Stuart's embodied and felt reactions to being "marginalized, humiliated, [and] belittled" in his prep school, and his disclosure profiling white supremacist acts thereof, as "a bigot is a bigot," demonstrate an immanent sense of the Other's feelings, which gives voice to our shared suffering. I am thus led by Stuart to co-experience dimensions of his embodied subjective feelings about racism that summons associative recollections in me.

This brief moment of empathy precipitated in a long and frank discussion on racial passing, which evolved into the topic of visible identity politics in the workplace. I asked Stuart if there were benefits to passing within his professional career. He explained that people in his workplace rarely made offhanded comments like those he heard at his prep school, because they "steered clear of the topic of race." Still, he spoke briefly of his resentment toward an African American female coworker, who unabashedly mentored only new lawyers of color and usually refused to help him by "making a smart ass remark, or saying that [she didn't] have time for [him]." Stuart explained that her actions were "unfair because I may need help too." Puzzled, and yet lured by these statements, I asked, "Does your office provide opportunities to lawyers of color to lead projects or advance?" He stated:

Well, no, and I understood that but it is how I feel. That's why I felt guilty about [my resentment]. I am a Jewish, white guy. My odds of succeeding are better; as a male, there are no glass ceilings. A white guy who is partner in a law firm is going to have more connections than an African American guy, who doesn't have the same options.

Stuart's response reveals the contradictory labels emphasized in the dynamic nature of white self-identity. His story resembles those told by whites who showed limited connection with members of their own racial group, but noted an awareness of being white when experiencing discomfort in interracial interactions.[25] As a member of a racially dominant and an oppressed ethnic group, Stuart experienced tensions of being violent and passive; having self-hatred, but resentment toward racialized others; and having associations with, and being isolated from white peers. There is yet another layer to Stuart's reflexive stance that certainly shows the ambiguity to which he embodies oppressed sensibilities of feeling victimized by his white peers, and a crisis of white masculinity operating in a schema of being victimized by the "unfair" mentoring practices of his African American female colleague. Although feeling victimized and privileged are contradictory ways of viewing one's racial status, these are byproducts of the "cycling dialectics" of white racial identity.[26] While Stuart admits to having systematic advantages that are unavailable to people of color and women, he also reinforces the limits of cross-racial empathy by suspending reflexivity on his resentment toward his colleague as merely a matter of "how [he] feels." While Stuart agonizes over his resentment, he disengages from it by turning to white male guilt that re-centers his racialized and gendered sense of self.

Conclusion

At issue here is Greg and Stuart's visceral sense of their racialized experiences as white men, shared with me, an African American interviewer, and the intercorporeal and multisensorial dance between us. After these interviews,

I contemplated what it meant not only to feel empathy with Greg's and Stuart's experiences of racism but to have an empathic presence, as their stories brought back my own somatic memories of racism. In this instance, I took the unusual step to understand and feel into how these white men felt, experienced, and perceived racist situations that directly impacted them. I tried to be fully mindful of the totality of their experiences of racism and their bodily movements and expressions by channeling how I *felt* in my own past experiences. We made eye contact. We nodded in agreement. We shared our stories. I consciously and cautiously made myself vulnerable to racial experiences of these men—something that I was uncomfortable with. While I felt, sensed, and anticipated their pain, I lamented in vexation and was attuned to the assemblages of senses disrupting opportunities to feel cross-racial empathy.

Despite my efforts to embody an empathic presence as a listener, I could not find it neither in my body nor soul to be a healing presence that inspires confidence in them.[27] It just didn't feel or seem right—historically and contextually speaking. Whiteness becomes more concrete through the eyes, ears, and even in the sensations of the flow of adrenaline in the bodies of people of color when they see white eyes glaze over in disbelief, or when whites open their mouths to interrupt when they are called out for being complicit in the system of white supremacy and privilege. In a recent book *Why I'm No Longer Talking to White People about Race*, Reni Eddo-Lodge, a black feminist, laments that whites who feel both attacked and silenced in conversations of race, ironically, lack empathy for people of color who spend their entire lives being marginalized and otherized.[28] Like many people of color, Eddo-Lodge feels the fatigue, emotional drifts, physical withdrawal, and eroding motivation when some white people engage in bodily habits of diminishing the experiences of people of color. The recurring feelings of physical and emotional exhaustion stick to the bodies of color, as we repeatedly encounter—as if it has been scripted and rehearsed—white people who become defensive when grappling with issues of racism. The challenges with empathetic racial crossings or the ability for whites to mirror and identify with experiences of people of color reveal the complex, tangled, and tortuous history of race and racism.

Intersubjective and interpersonal empathy is felt and sensed through the process of entrainment, an ongoing attempt to create synchrony of rhythms in interaction, and of feeling with and inhabiting the world through the other's body. The point is not whether empathy is achieved or not, but the fact that empathy requires somatic and sensorial participation, which underpins the potentiality of empathetic connection. Such attempt is of course fraught with failures and disharmony—the history of racism is the history of negating the possibility of empathic feeling-with across racial lines. Feeling empathy in cross-racial interaction is more than sharing experiences of racism, but a process of co-generating somatic and visceral feelings, and co-experiencing the informative flow of embodied rhythms that shape deeper meanings of these experiences. In considering empathy in cross-racial encounters, we must first tend to registers of our body, the somato-affective knowledge and labor that establish the possibility of feeling with and sensing into one another.

7

Conclusion

Pedagogy of the Sensuous

In the poignant narrative of a racially revealing moment, Shannon Sullivan recounts a classroom interaction where she addressed the stereotype about African American men as sexual predators, to which a white female student responded and insisted as follows: "But I *am* scared of black men! If I pass one on the street at night, I can't help it. I tense up and get knots in my stomach."[1] The female student's viscerally felt fear—the gut reaction to the sight of a black man on the dark street—"proved" the danger of black masculinity: "Since nothing is more real or irrefutable than felt physiological responses— unchosen and unwilled, after all—then her body's alarmed response to black men means that they *are* frightening."[2] The hegemonic power of racism is solidified when one's racist attitudes and behaviors are experienced as a gut reaction—a visceral reflex, an automatic and unintentional reaction of fear, distrust, discomfort, or disgust in response to the presence of the racialized Other. Beyond rhetorical and discursive constructions of racial stereotypes, racist fear and hate run through the veins, hearts, and guts of living human beings, shaping their daily habits and orientations toward others.[3] For racism to live on, not only does it have to be reproduced *ideologically* but also it must be *habituated into the bodies*, forming a collective and regenerative community of bodies that feel, move, and resonate with racialized and racist sensescapes.

Experiences of race and racism are accompanied by, and materialized through somatic, affective, and emotional sensations felt and sensed on and through our lived bodies. In Sullivan's anecdote, the idea of racial stereotype about black male criminality becomes irrefutable not because it is logically persuasive or statistically convincing, but because the sensation that accompanies the sight of black men (i.e., knots in the stomach) is materially and viscerally felt by the white female student. Even if the fear of black men itself is something she learned through racially biased socialization, once the gut reaction becomes automatic and unquestioned, the viscerally felt fear *is* the evidence of black male criminality. Even if the fear itself is the product of a racist stereotype, once the association between an idea (black male criminality) and embodied affect (fear) is established, the fear now feeds and reifies the stereotype. When a racist gut reaction is habituated into the body, it requires little persuasion for people to hold on to its "truth." Such visceral confirmation of the racist stereotype—I fear you, therefore you are dangerous—naturalizes black male criminality and reaffirms the normativity of white female sensibility. As black male bodies are marked as dangerous, white female bodies assemble into a fearful subject. At the intersection of racialized and gendered sensescapes, black men cannot *not* be dangerous, so long as white women cannot *not* be afraid of them. Racist societies produce a relation of sensing, of the bodies that are sensed as dangerous, and the bodies that are authorized, socially and historically, to sense and authenticate the danger of the racialized Other. To question the relations of power, then, we must interrogate the relations of sensing.

Sullivan claims that "like most contemporary white ignorance/knowledge, [the white female student's] affective 'knowledge' that black men are threatening operated primarily on a non-cognitive, bodily level."[4] What the white female student feels—and how it registers in her body—functions not only as the product of a racist stereotype but also as the somato-affective knowledge that confirms her previously internalized racist beliefs. Even if the fear emerged after (or because of) the stereotype, now the fear actively authenticates the racist belief. When she feels afraid, the fear viscously sticks to the black male bodies as if the black male bodies emanate such fear. The materiality of the bodily feelings—the raw, physiological reaction of being tense and feeling knots in the stomach—viscerally substantiates the racist stereotype.

In Chapter 2, we discussed Martin Berger's idea that the visual experience of race retroactively confirms and materially verifies the preexisting racist beliefs.[5] Echoing his claim, we argue more broadly that sensory experiences are deployed to materially and co-constitutively substantiate preexisting ideas and beliefs about race. The social and ideological construction of race *requires* the somatosensory and visceral feelings that bring to life the arbitrary and fictive object called race. Race and racism do not simply organize and discipline our sensory perceptions and experiences; race and racism actively produce somatosensory and affective experiences (i.e., fear, gut reaction) that viscerally legitimate racist beliefs and racialized practices. As a hegemonic social construct, race must be registered and reregistered into the collective bodies and somatic imaginations to naturalize its existence.

The fact that race is experienced as real through felt sensations and feelings does not mean the senses are simply fooled and distorted when we perceive race. Rather, it means somatic labor and sensorial engagements play a vital role in the construction of racialized relations of power. What one feels physically and affectively—even if they are not explicitly named, claimed, or identified—underscore the particular subject position and worldview one comes to assume as a racial and social subject. Robin DiAngelo uses the term "white fragility" to describe the recurring patterns of behaviors observed when white people are confronted with issues of racism and privilege, including anger, guilt, fear, anxiety, defensiveness, denial, and silence.[6] DiAngelo provides numerous examples of how white bodies literally shut down to avoid the discomfort of talking about racism. It is a gut reaction of whiteness induced by being called out for one's racial privilege and complicity. The gut reaction is a defense mechanism to preserve the status quo and recover from the racial accusation that disorients the normative bodily orientation of whiteness. When one is in the position of privilege, the world is crafted around their sensibilities and comfort. To be called out for one's complicity in racial oppression disrupts the somatosensory underpinning of whiteness, a bodily and affective foundation of white racial identity rooted in mobility, freedom, moral uprightness, meritocracy, and individuality. White fragility may be understood as a bodily sensation of what whiteness feels like, or how whiteness reverberates within privileged bodies.

Race scholarship emphasizes the fact that people of color have been historically marginalized and objectified within the system that privileges and humanizes white people.[7] While the senses are in many ways skewed and manipulated by and for racism, it also remains true that the senses are the medium of possibility and the foundation of subjectivity and intersubjectivity. What tends to be underestimated in this process is that those who are reduced to an object still feel and sense such objectification. Ta-Nehisi Coates writes,

> But all our phrasing—race relations, racial chasm, racial justice, racial profiling, white privilege, even white supremacy—serves to obscure that racism is a visceral experience, that it dislodges brains, blocks airways, rips muscle, extracts organs, cracks bones, breaks teeth. You must never look away from this. You must always remember that the sociology, the history, the economics, the graphs, the charts, the regressions all land, with great violence, upon the body.[8]

Coates repeatedly reminds his son (and readers) not to look away or forget that his body is the ground zero of racism. For racialized subjects, racial embodiment emerges in a seemingly paradoxical condition in which one's existential subjectivity is rooted in their awareness of their objectification: I feel my objectification, therefore, I am. For those who are socially marginalized, the visceral sensations and bodily feelings are the daily reminder of their existence both as an object and as subject. They continue to feel, even the numbness of their dispossessed subjectivity, beyond and underneath the words that betray or silence their existence. That is perhaps why Coates reminds his son of the visceral nature of racism: while his body is the target of racism, it is also the primordial foundation of his subjectivity, agency, and freedom. While our senses are cultivated, dominated, and colonized by the violence of racism, our embodied senses viscerally draw attention to the living, feeling body as the sentient foundation of one's humanity.

The premise of this book—race is felt and sensed—emerged not from a theoretical or conceptual concern, but from our embodied, lived *feelings* as racialized subjects. In our somatic reflections on racialized encounters, our approach was to let our bodily feelings and sensorial experiences speak for themselves—to authorize and authenticate the sentient bodies as subjects of sensuous knowledge. Through somatically reflecting on the felt-qualities and movements of racialized encounters, we came to understand the sensorial, affective, and kinesthetic dimensions of race. Racial embodiment must be theorized not only in terms of its visual construction but as a lived body that feels, senses, moves, acts, and interacts with other bodies within a given social environment. The lived body is both an affective medium of subjective experience and a site where power relations are habituated. Embodied experiences and bodily sensations are a source of knowledge for critically understanding, and potentially transforming, the relations of sensing that uphold and substantiate the broader and more systematic relations of power.

The Prosthetic Relation between Race and the Senses

Throughout the book, we engaged in somatic work of reflecting on how race is felt and sensed into being. Far from being merely a visible category of social difference, race and racial differences materialize across the shifting boundaries between felt resonance and dissonance that are simultaneously affective, material, and visceral at the intersubjective and intercorporeal levels. The racial reality is saturated with visual, tactile, kinesthetic, auditory, olfactory, gustatory, and other felt-qualities that appeal to our senses, constantly renewing and reproducing particular sensory assemblages. Our phenomenological and somatosensory descriptions of racialization and racism illuminate that multiple bodily senses are engaged in racialized interactions and experiences, and such embodied multisensory feelings are integral to the social construction of race.

The term "social construction" often connotes a sense of being artificial, or something that is made up. Our analyses of the relationship between race and the senses, however, reveal the artificiality of race not in terms of being false or nonexistent, but in the sense that race functions like a prosthetic or artificial extension, something that extends or amplifies the bodily senses.[9] The social life of race is prosthetic in nature, in that once race is incorporated into the sensory apparatus—the interactive system of sensory order (social/cultural ways of feeling) and feeling bodies (lived subjects)—race works coextensively with the sensing/feeling bodies to sustain its life. As a prosthetic technology (of oppression), race comes to life and becomes real in our lived experiences by racializing not only the visible surface of bodies but also the embodied senses. Felt bodily sensations create a viscous relation between the racist idea/practice and the embodied senses. Race, as a social construct, is artificial not because the very idea of race was invented, but because race prosthetically extends the senses, producing the relations of sensing and feeling that reflect and reify broader social relations of power.

The genius of racism is that it targets the skin (and its color), because the skin is not only a visible marker of differences but also a feeling organ. Racialization produces a prosthetic skin over the racialized body: we may call this a second skin. The second skin becomes a prosthetic organ through which racialized subjects feel the world. Racialization prosthetically extends one's skin, from having the biological skin to living in the social skin. Racialized subjects live with a form of skin consciousness: one is highly conscious of the implications of one's skin (color) in various social contexts, while the skin itself actively feels the touch, texture, and heat of racially charged interactions and spaces. Racialized consciousness resides in the skin, covering the whole body with a layer of racial awareness. For racialized subjects, the skin consciousness becomes a bodily organ for assessing risk, affirming racial solidarity, sensing belonging, feeling "out of place," or buffering microaggressions. The second skin prosthetically extends and inhibits ways of feeling, moving, and relating within and across racial boundaries. To live in a racialized society means to live and breathe through the second skin that senses and responds to the geography of racialized bodies.

To argue that race is felt and sensed into existence speaks to the centrality of our lived, sentient, and feeling bodies that actively participate in materializing social reality. The social construction of race is simultaneously the social and historical construction of the feeling body. The body learns how to extend itself through the racialized senses in a racialized social environment. The body's sensuous participation is not a one-way street: race works coextensively with our bodies and senses, transfiguring our bodily senses and sensibilities. What we feel through our senses make race and racialization viscous: a social object (such as race) sticks to the body as felt sensations activate and materialize the animate life of the social object. Our sentient and sensuous bodies are where the assembling forces of race collide and make lasting impressions. What our bodies feel, then, is political. The feeling body is a repository of social and cultural knowledge accumulated through bodily habituation and repetition.

Arun Saldanha pointedly argues that "the concept of race is not for taxonomic ordering, but for studying the movements between human bodies, things, and their changing environment."[10] He theorizes race in terms of viscosity— the ways in which certain bodies, places, and ideas gradually stick together into aggregates. For example, whiteness is about "the sticky connections between property, privilege, and a paler skin"[11] that are held together for generations through policies and practices such as anti-miscegenation laws, housing segregation, and family inheritance. Saldanha argues that "race is a nonnecessary and irreducible effect of the ways those bodies themselves interact with each other and their physical environment."[12] That is, *what race is* shifts and changes according to the ways in which the bodies interact and aggregate. Racialized housing segregation, for example, creates proximity among certain types of classed and raced bodies (aggregation), while driving other bodies geographically and physically away from them (segregation). Saldanha argues that "battling against racism is not a question of denying race, but of cultivating its energies against the stickiness of racial segregation."[13] Extending Saldanha's approach, we emphasize the role of somatosensory experiences and visceral feelings in creating the viscosity of race. If race is an effect of how bodies and objects are held together, such viscosity is felt by the body, and the viscous sensation further congeals the stickiness of racial segregation and aggregation. The viscosity of racial segregation is not an objective phenomenon on the map, but it materializes as a felt experience of how the bodies (are allowed to) move within and across streets, blocks, and neighborhoods. Somatosensory experiences mediate and materialize the viscosity of racial formation.

Pedagogy of the Sensuous

It is far more difficult to dispel *how race is felt as real* than to debunk *how race is thought to be real*. As professors of intercultural communication, we have asked the following question to undergraduate students numerous times in our classrooms: *Is race social construct or biological fact?* In a classroom activity, we instruct students to go to the right side of the classroom if they think race is a social construction, or to move to the left side if they think race is biological. In a typical classroom of twenty-five to thirty students, most students appear a bit stunned by the question, as if the answer is so obvious that they never even thought about it before. Some students choose to walk toward the side of social construction—mostly because they read the assigned chapter—while still seeming a bit unsure about their choice. Those students know they are right—because the textbook said so!—but cannot shed a hint of doubt in their minds. Other students walk to the side of seeing race as a biological entity, including a few students of color, who wonder if this is a trick question or if the real answer is "both/and." We follow up with questions as to why they chose either side, evolving into a heated debate on why and how race is a social construction.

For those students who believe race is biological, their argument usually focuses on the fact that visible racial markers (i.e., skin color, hair texture, and the eye shape) are what we inherited from our parents *biologically*. For them, physical features are the material evidence of racial differences, while those who view race as a social construction argue back by saying these physical features are only meaningful in certain social contexts, pointing out the arbitrary nature of racial markers. When students choose the side of biology, they are not necessarily speaking from the perspective of genetic science or even scientific racism. Rather, the term "biological" captures more closely their perceptions of racial differences that are seemingly self-evident, permanent, commonsensical, and therefore registered as "natural." The mantra of "race is socially constructed" fails to capture more seemingly intuitive and commonsensical perceptions of racial differences. Such felt, yet unspoken, ways of sensing differences underpin racialized encounters and cross-racial interactions.

The progressive education on race and identity politics in the past several decades have not fully addressed the visceral, affective, and felt dimensions of race and racism that slip through the cracks of symbolic labels and linguistic interventions. Or more precisely, negative feelings regarding race—anything that may potentially be labeled as racist—have been treated as something that people shouldn't feel, or simply as a by-product of incorrect or skewed understanding of racial others. David A. Granger rightly critiques the reliance on discursive logic to combat power relations where "the subtle visceral, 'felt' dimensions of racism (as opposed to more overt feelings) . . . [are treated] as merely incidental phenomena."[14] The discursive logic of justice and equality condemns racism, while leaving the visceral feelings and pre-reflective habits suppressed or unproblematized. The assumption is that we can overcome racism with our mighty cognition and enlightened mind, while neglecting or underestimating the reach of racialized habituation and sedimentation in our bodies. Racialized perceptual habits, however, are sedimented in the ways of feeling and sensing self, others, and the world. As Richard Shusterman posits, somatic norms materialize and maintain dominant ideologies by encoding them into taken-for-granted bodily habits.[15] Similarly, Helen Ngo suggests racism emerges not only in the intentional acts of individuals but also more profoundly and "insidiously" in the register of bodily habits.[16] Given the somatic nature of racial learning, it is highly revealing that the idea of racial colorblindness emerged as a loophole of anti-racist efforts, allowing people to hold onto their visceral racism while showcasing their enlightened minds and skilled use of identity jargons.

When the sensorial phenomenology of race and racism is concerned, it is useful to think about racism in terms of felt bodily resonance and dissonance. The logic of racism resonates with those who hold racist and white supremacist beliefs, not merely cognitively and ideologically, but viscerally and physiologically. Racial hegemony operates subtly yet persuasively through felt resonance, rather than logic or reason. The lived body registers and remembers the feelings of resonance and dissonance, comfort and discomfort, hate and love, and "us versus them." Racialization and racism produce and regulate the felt resonance and dissonance between familiarity and foreignness, proximity and distance, affinity and otherness, inclusion and exclusion, as well as moral uprightness and corruptness. Such gut feeling is not a natural reflex, but a bodily reminder of implicitly habituated ways of feeling about racial others. Gut reactions reveal the history of racial embodiment and racialized bodily habituation—the history of somatic work involved in producing the racialized relations of feeling and sensing.

The visceral nature of racial politics is deeply entrenched and heightened in the age of social media, where viral posts and hashtags can be used to orchestrate public opinion and polarized ideologies. Social media such as Facebook and Twitter create a hyper-connected social environment deprived of certain sensory input, particularly the senses of touch, taste, smell, as well as spatial and thermal information present in face-to-face interactions. These sensory dimensions are usually in the background of our conscious experiences. In face-to-face communication, what makes social interactions fulfilling or meaningful is not merely the content of messages we exchange verbally, but the experience of being together, sharing a physical space, feeling one another's bodily presence, listening to the tone of voice, smelling the scent in the air, or experiencing mutual recognition through eye contact. Intersubjective senses of self are grounded in these shared somatosensory experiences. Interactions on social media, by contrast, are mediated primarily by visual images, written texts, and digitally mediated sounds that severely curtail those background sensations. People bring a "body" into digital communication by using emojis, emoticons, and GIFs to supplement nonverbal gestures and facial expressions to text-based exchanges on a flat digital screen. Drowning in floods of information that rapidly change the emotional landscape of interpersonal interactions, we still yearn for material experiences to ground our cognitive and emotional processing of information. Digital culture creates a particular sensory ecology that subtly yet materially undermines direct somatosensory sensations that ground the senses of self and other. In the age of social media, individuals in front of a digital device are now tasked with the labor of feeling—whether it is hate, prejudice, love, joy, solidarity, friendship, or patriotism—in order to tangibly engage with others in virtual communities. Digital culture requires a unique form of somatic work in which we align, perform, and experience identities, ideologies, and belonging through digital behaviors and associated somato-affective feelings. In such context, hateful or xenophobic messages may produce (and require) far greater somato-affective reaction (or resonance) because the body is already deprived of various direct somatosensory experiences. Extremist views and populist ideologies stick and thrive on social media, because they provoke sensations and feelings that appease and potentially remedy the sensory deprivation experienced by digitally mediated bodies and identities.

Anti-racist efforts risk greater backlash and resistance if anti-racist education suppresses—rather than recognizes and acknowledges—the racist gut reaction and racialized bodily habits and impulses. As we have demonstrated throughout this book, race extends its prosthetic capacity not only into our minds but also onto our senses, habits, and embodiment. Anti-racist work must include the reorientation and re-habituation of our bodily-ways-of-being-with-others. Powerful ideologies both compel and require visceral confirmation (or disconfirmation). What we feel—individually and collectively, historically and presently, as well as emotionally and sensorially—matters greatly. Bodily senses and sensations not only materialize abstract ideas into concrete experiences but also hold together certain bodies, feelings, ideas, and collectivities.[17] The tactile metaphor of race as a viscous material that engages the intermingled senses reveals the animate life of race as a social object. This metaphor enables a sensory exploration into the texture, weight, gravity, and force of race that leave varying impressions on the skin. Rather than dismissing these visceral and bodily feelings, we must attend to these feelings as pedagogical resources for anti-racist education.

Feeling the Way Forward

The question of "what to do about racism"—after the cognitive and intellectualist remedy fell short—has been variously addressed by philosophers of race in terms of existential and ethical responsibilities. Alia Al-Saji, for example, proposes the notion of affective hesitation as a way of interrupting racializing vision and perceptual habits that naturalize racist perception.[18] To interrupt racializing perception means to slow down and recognize the habituated ways of seeing and perceiving the racialized Other. If racist perceptions become reified through the gut reaction of "I cannot see or feel otherwise," anti-racism must cultivate mindful and proactive suspension of such affective bodily habits.[19] Similarly, Helen Ngo argues that passive racist habits are actively held by racist subjects and calls attention to the responsibility of changing one's racist habits.[20] Gail Weiss foregrounds the existential responsibilities of white subjects to reflect on and recognize racialized habits and prejudices,[21] while Danielle Petherbridge focuses on the affective relationality as a primordial form of sociality that can disrupt racializing perceptions.[22] The proposal for anti-racist habits and subjectivity based on ethical and existential responsibilities, however, risks reinforcing an assumed superiority of the mind in which an abstract (and existential) mind can somehow intervene the bodily and somatic habits of racism. That is, locating the virus of racism in the habituated bodies and seeking intervention into bodily habits subtly reinscribes the subordinated status of the body in relation to the entity (i.e., the mind, the ethical act) we presume to be capable of disrupting racist habits.

If the myriad dimensions of sociality and relationality are learned through the senses, we contend it is also through the senses that oppressive or hegemonic habits can be transformed. The process of loosening or eliminating the viscosity of race requires the same, if not greater, amount of sensorial and somatic work. To unlearn racism means to learn to stick differently, to touch and be touched by the world differently, to negotiate distance and proximity differently, to find different cords and rhythms that resonate, and to extend our bodies differently to one another. The act of walking hand-in-hand in the 1963 March on Washington, for example, was not merely a symbolic gesture of multiracial solidarity, but a form of somatic work by literally extending the arms toward one another, sharing the touch and warmth of the hands, walking in coordinated speed, and marking the historic movement through the moving bodies.[23] As Danielle Petherbridge posits, the rupture of racist habits and perceptions must take place not only at the structural level but also at the level of embodied affectivity.[24] The senses are themselves heuristic and pedagogical—the sentient body is itself existential in its nature. Shusterman suggests that somatic awareness—exploring bodily habits and feelings, which are already firmly established in institutional and dominant norms—is key to addressing visceral feelings of prejudice and hostility within oppressive social conditions:[25]

> Much racial and ethnic hostility is not the product of logical thought but of deep prejudices that are somatically expressed or embodied in vague but disagreeable feelings that typically lie beneath the level of explicit consciousness. Such prejudices and feelings thus resist correction by mere discursive arguments for tolerance, which can be accepted on the rational level without changing the visceral grip of prejudice. We often deny that we have such prejudices because we do not realize that we feel them, and the first step to controlling or expunging them is to develop the somatic awareness to recognize them in ourselves.[26]

Habits are more difficult to notice and undo than correcting an illogic of prejudice and discrimination based on the "proper" and more enlightened structure of reasoning. From the somatic and sensorial perspective, it is not enough—and even potentially counterproductive—to teach justice and equity as a social logic or principle. Rather, justice and equity must be habituated into the bodies by cultivating the bodies that feel dissonance, disorientation, or even disgust in the face of injustice and inequity. Addressing racist habits of white ignorance as historical bodily sedimentations, Gail Weiss argues that within anti-racist projects, sedimentation is not only part of the problem in showing how racist inclinations are historically situated but also part of the solution for the future because anti-racist habits must be habituated and sedimented at both the individual and community level.[27] It is not enough, then, to break the "bad habits" of racism; we must cultivate alternative habits and sedimentations of perception, senses, and intersubjectivity that are generative and regenerative of equity, community, and freedom.

Following Shusterman's notion of somaesthetics, Granger argues anti-racist education must entail a form of "reflective somatic education" that improves our "somatic mindfulness."[28] That is, we must be introspective of our bodily sensations and habits in interracial encounters, identifying "some more prevalent (if not universal) bodily responses to encounters with racial 'others'—for instance, avoidance of eye contact, maintenance of physical distance, constriction of muscles and other viscera, and alterations in breathing—that trigger or reinforce (to the extent that they are already present) prejudicial or discriminatory patterns of speaking, thinking, and acting."[29] The primary purpose of reflective somatic education is to take heed of the body to the extent that somatic reflection itself becomes a regular practice.[30] The goal is not to "correct" racist habits or "command" the body to perceive in certain ways, but to cultivate a collectivity of social and sentient bodies that are somatically and sensorially mindful of the racialized relations of sensing and feeling. To transform the relations of power, we must cultivate alternative relations of sensing.

It is important to emphasize that the reflective somatic awareness for anti-racism is not about individual efforts, but a collective and interactive endeavor. It is not a goal, but a process. There is no arbitrary or idealistic marker of achievement. It is not about acknowledging one's privilege—a performative act that has become widely common as a qualifier in conversations about race. Rather, it is a cultivation of ongoing and evolving awareness to attend to the ways in which our bodies and objects stick together and get stuck; to examine the viscous habituation of ideas and practices; and to experiment with alternative ways of sticking together and extending ourselves to one another. It is about coming to terms with the ways in which racism has been somatically habituated into our bodies. It is about taking the embodied senses seriously in understanding the social and ideological construction of reality. It is about using all of our senses to imagine, inquire, and relate to the experiences of others. It is about extending our senses to design a community that facilitates sensorial well-being. Critical sensorial awareness should be cultivated as a form of intercultural competency, ethical relation, and moral foundation.

Beyond Race and the Senses

Perhaps one of the biggest challenges in social and cultural theorizing is how to study something without murdering it or halting its life into a still object. More than any other object of scholarly investigation, the body presents a great obstacle in this regard. How do we theorize, comprehend, and give symbolic meaning to the body without taking away its inherent characteristic—to be alive, to feel, to change, and to move? The body is always already in excess of itself. Any attempt to form a unified knowledge about the body ends up feeling deeply disembodied. In this book, we explored the question of racial embodiment by highlighting its sensorial and phenomenological dimensions to theorize the bodies-in-motion as dynamic and sensuous phenomena. This approach was not merely an intellectual project, but an attempt to reclaim embodied subjectivity in otherwise objectifying and dehumanizing experiences of race and racism.

While our focus in this book was on the relations between race and the senses, more research and theorizing must be done to address other intersecting identities and subject positions, including but not limited to gender, sexuality, class, ability, citizenship, and religion. From the sensorial and phenomenological perspectives, the exploration into the sensuous content of one's identity is highly intriguing. This means to approach identity not in terms of the grid of intersecting categories, but in terms of the felt content of assuming and living in a social body with multiple dimensions and layers. The category (i.e., black, woman, and middle class) always has its sensuous content; or more precisely, the identity category sustains itself as an aggregate of its sensuous content. Felt sensations are necessarily elusive, ephemeral, and often escapes linguistic fixity. At the same time, felt sensations linger in the bodies, memories, and viscously remain within us. A "self" emerges as an ongoing accumulation of lived experiences and sensations etched into one's muscle memories and daily habits. In the end, a "self" is a sticky subject, an assemblage of felt experiences, memories, and other lived bodies that make impressions on our bodies.

The point is not to essentialize certain identities into certain feelings, but to reveal the processes through which a "self" coheres into a subject through recurring or remarkable experiences and feelings. We may begin by theorizing identity not as a category (or a set of categories), but as emergent or recurring sequences of felt experiences that aggregate, however elusively, into a "self," "nation," or "race." We may set identity theorizing in motion, literally and metaphorically, by attending to the bodies that feel, move, and collide within the intersecting matrix of power. What would it look like to theorize identities and subjectivities not in terms of the intersecting grid of identity categories, but as an aggregate or assemblage of sensorial experiences? What other categories, subject positions, and senses of belonging are possible if we approached "difference" as sensuous materiality rather than a predetermined category? How would it change the possibilities of understanding the Other? How would it enable more empathetic connections across the boundaries of difference? These questions seem increasingly important to address today, as the gut reaction to return to nationalistic, xenophobic, and ethnocentric collectivity gains greater appeal around the globe.

Starting at a very young age, we internalize and incorporate social values and norms into our lived embodiment. Parents and caretakers spend much time telling and guiding their young children what not to touch, lick, or ingest; how to share toys and space; how loudly or quietly they should speak; how to reciprocate hugs and greetings; how to pay attention to cars on the street, or recognize danger in certain neighborhoods; or how to name colors, flavors, and emotions. In essence, we all learn how to extend our bodies and senses into the social and material world, as the world extends its shapes, textures, weight, and meaning on our bodies. Social norms and cultural values enable, regulate, or discipline the possibilities of one's sensorial embodiment. What is perceptible and feel-able is both enabled and inhibited by the way we utilize and cultivate our senses. That is, the sensuous body is always coextensive with the social and material environment.

As human beings, we absorb information, internalize knowledge, and become part of the lived environment through our multiple senses. The lived body Merleau-Ponty wrote about is not just a chunk of flesh that moves, but an open field of embodied sensory experiences that make a multitude of colors, textures, tastes, scents, and sounds perceptible and "experienceable." Race seems to play upon such bodily sensory openness and closes it down. If Merleau-Ponty's corporeal schema opened up our embodiment to the world of bodily knowing, Fanon showed how racialized bodily schema is completely skewed and made numb, in that people of color are racially disembodied and do not own their bodily schema.[31] Race continues to exert its hegemonic presence when we close down our corporeal schema into an apparatus of racialized senses. Racism is not only a paradigm of corrupt reason but, more fundamentally, a paradigm of corrupt senses. In order to disrupt the oppressive sensory apparatus of race, we must cultivate a phenomenological and sensorial awareness of our racialized perceptual habits through which various sensory experiences are made socially meaningful.

Attending to the sensuous and sensorial is inherently pedagogical. We want to conclude our book with a practical and pedagogical suggestion to take our senses seriously and sensuously—to feel race until it is no longer feel-able in habituated, normative, and hegemonic ways. It means to (re)encounter race as a strange object, carefully examining the texture, movement, weight, and gravity in its own right as race manifests, extends, or inhibits one's sensuous embodiment. This process means to pay somatic attention to our bodies-in-interaction-with-others and observe the muscles that contract, the postures that orient us toward one another, the affectivity felt in the space, the sound of familiarity and foreignness, or the contours of the face that appear through the exchange of gaze. The point is not to stop ourselves from feeling race or to feel race differently (or more justly or humanely); rather, it is to feel race more deeply and complexly, in its current and most immediate and intimate manifestation, attending somatically to the every detail and nuance of its sensations. Only with such critical somatic and sensorial awareness can we begin to loosen the viscosity of racial sensory assemblages that have been viscerally held together for centuries.

NOTES

Chapter 1

1 Somatic work is defined as a self-reflexive process that involves sensing (somatic perception) and making sense (semiotic interpretation). It is "a process whereby a somatic perception undergoes a reflexive interpretation" shaped by the "somatic rules" that regulate one's socio-somatic perception and its interpretation. Dennis D. Waskul and Phillip Vannini, "Smell, Odor, and Somatic Work: Sense-making and Sensory Management," *Social Psychology Quarterly* 71, no. 1 (2008): 58. Also see, Phillip Vannini, Dennis Waskul, and Simon Gottschalk, *The Senses in Self, Society, and Culture: A Sociology of the Senses* (New York: Routledge, 2012), 18–21.

2 Thomas J. Csordas, "Somatic Mode of Attention," *Cultural Anthropology* 8, no. 2 (1993): 135–56; Kathryn Linn Geurts, "Consciousness as 'Feeling in the Body': A West African Theory of Embodiment, Emotion and the Making of Mind," in *Empire of the Senses: The Sensual Culture Reader*, ed. David Howes (Oxford: Berg, 2005), 164–78.

3 Brian Massumi, *Parables for the Virtual: Movement, Affect, Sensation* (Durham: Duke University, 2002); Arun Saldanha, *Psychedelic White: Goa Trance and the Viscosity of Race* (Minneapolis: University of Minnesota, 2007).

4 For critique of social constructionism, see Ian Hacking, *The Social Construction of What?* (Cambridge: Harvard University Press, 1999). For critique of social construction of race as tautology, see Barnor Hesse "Racialized Modernity: An Analytics of White Mythologies," *Ethnic and Racial Studies* 30 (2007): 643–63.

5 Kyoo Lee, "Why Asian Female Stereotypes Matter to All: Beyond Black and White, East and West," *Critical Philosophy of Race* 1, no. 1 (2013): 89.

6 Constance Classen, *The Deepest Touch: A Cultural History of Touch* (Urbana: University of Illinois, 2012); Csordas, "Somatic Mode"; Kathryn Linn Geurts, *Culture and the Senses: Bodily Ways of Knowing in an African Community* (Berkeley: University of California, 2002); Asia Friedman, "Toward a Sociology of Perception: Sight, Sex, and Gender," *Cultural Sociology* 5, no. 2 (2011): 187–206; David Howes, ed., *Empire of the Senses: The Sensual Culture Reader* (Oxford: Berg, 2005); David Howes, *Sensual Relations: Engaging in the Senses in Culture and Social Theory* (Ann Arbor: The University of Michigan, 2003); David Howes and Constance Classen, *Ways of Sensing: Understanding the Senses in Society* (New York: Routledge, 2014); David Le Breton, *Sensing the World: An Anthropology of the Senses*, trans. Carmen

Ruschiensky (London: Bloomsbury Academic, 2017); Paul Stoller, *Sensuous Scholarship* (Philadelphia: University of Pennsylvania, 1997); Sarah Pink, *Doing Sensory Ethnography* (Los Angeles: Sage, 2015); Michel Serres, *The Five Senses: A Philosophy of Mingled Bodies*, trans. Margaret Sankey and Peter Cowley (London: Bloomsbury Academic, 2016); Vannini et al., *The Senses in Self*.

7   Mark Smith, *How Race Is Made: Slavery, Segregation, and the Senses* (Chapel Hill: The University of North Carolina Press, 2006).

8   Asia Friedman, "'There Are Two People at Work That I'm Fairly Certain Are Black': Uncertainty and Deliberative Thinking in Blind Race Attribution," *The Sociological Quarterly* 57 (2016): 437–461; Osagie K. Obasogie, *Blinded by Sight: Seeing Race through the Eyes of the Blind* (Stanford: Stanford University, 2014).

9   Deborah Poole, *Vision, Race, and Modernity: A Visual Economy of the Andean World* (Princeton: Princeton University, 1997).

10   Signithia Fordham, "'Those Loud Black Girls': (Black) Women, Silence, and Gender 'Passing' in the Academy," *Anthropology and Education Quarterly* 24, no. 1 (1993): 3–32.

11   Joy L. Lei, "(Un)necessary Toughness?: Those 'Loud Black Girls' and Those 'Quiet Asian Boys,'" *Anthropology & Education Quarterly* 34, no. 2 (2003): 158–81.

12   Nicky Hudson, "Towards Multi-Sensory Research: Acoustic Space, Racialisation and Whiteness," *Journal of Research in Nursing* 13, no. 2 (2008): 113–22.

13   Alice Ashton Filmer, "Bilingual Belonging and the Whiteness of (Standard) English(es)," *Qualitative Inquiry* 13, no. 6 (2007): 747–65; Geoff Mann, "Why Does Country Music Sound White? Race and the Voice of Nostalgia," *Ethnic and Racial Studies* 31, no. 1 (2008): 73–100.

14   Jennifer Lynn Stoever, *The Sonic Color Line: Race and the Cultural Politics of Listening* (New York: New York University, 2016).

15   Kelvin E. Y. Low, *Scent and Scent-sibilities: Smell and Everyday Life Experiences* (Newcastle-upon-Tyne: Cambridge Scholars Publishing, 2009); Martin F. Manalansan IV, "Immigrant Lives and the Politics of Olfaction in the Global City," in *The Smell Culture Reader*, ed. Jim Drobnick (Oxford: Berg, 2006), 41–52.

16   Laura U. Marks, *The Skin of the Film: Intercultural Cinema, Embodiment, and the Senses* (Durham: Duke University, 2000).

17   Alex Rhys-Taylor, *Food and Multiculture: A Sensory Ethnography of East London* (London: Bloomsbury Academic, 2017).

18   Robert Ji-Song Ku, *Dubious Gastronomy: The Cultural Politics of Eating Asian in the USA* (Honolulu: University of Hawaii, 2014); Emily Walmsley, "Race, Place and Taste: Making Identities Through Sensory Experience in Ecuador," *Etnofoor* 18, no. 1 (2005): 43–60.

19   Sachi Sekimoto, "Race and the Senses: Toward Articulating the Sensory Apparatus of Race," *Critical Philosophy of Race* 6, no. 1 (2018): 82–100.

20 George Yancy, *Black Bodies, White Gazes: The Continuing Significance of Race* (Lanham: Rowman and Littlefield, 2008).

21 Sara Ahmed, "A Phenomenology of Whiteness," *Feminist Theory* 8 (2007): 149–68; Sara Ahmed, *On Being Included: Racism and Diversity in Institutional Life* (Durham: Duke University, 2012); Linda Martín Alcoff, "Towards an Embodiment of Racial Phenomenology," *Radical Philosophy* 95 (1999): 15–26; Linda Martín Alcoff, *Visible Identities: Race, Gender, and the Self* (New York; Oxford University, 2006); Frantz Fanon, *Black Skin, White Masks*, trans. Charles Lam Markmann (New York: Grove, 1967); Saldanha, *Psychedelic White*; Iris Marion Young, *On Female Body Experience: "Throwing Like a Girl" and Other Essays* (New York: Oxford University, 2005).

22 Emily S. Lee, *Living Alterities: Phenomenology, Embodiment, and Race* (Albany: SUNY Press, 2014); Helen Ngo, *The Habits of Racism: A Phenomenology of Racism and Racialized Embodiment* (Lanham: Lexington Books, 2012).

23 Friedman, "Toward a Sociology of Perception," 200.

24 Asia Friedman, "Perceptual Construction: Rereading *The Social Construction of Reality* through the Sociology of the Senses," *Cultural Sociology* 10, no. 1 (2016): 79.

25 Howes, *Sensual Relations*, xi.

26 David A. Granger, "Somaesthetics and Racism: Toward an Embodied Pedagogy of Difference," *Journal of Aesthetic Education* 44, no. 3 (2010): 78.

27 Friedman, "Perceptual Construction," 82.

28 Janine Young Kim, "Racial Emotions and the Feeling of Equality," *University of Colorado Law Review* 87 (2016): 438–96.

29 Shannon Sullivan, "The Hearts and Guts of White People: Ethics, Ignorance, and the Physiology of White Racism," *Journal of Religious Ethics* 42, no. 4 (2014): 591–611.

30 Davide Panagia, *The Political Life of Sensation* (Durham: Duke University, 2009), prologue, Kindle.

31 Vannini et al., *The Senses in Self*, 20; emphasis in original.

32 Marks, *The Skin of Film*, 123.

33 Alexis Shotwell, *Knowing Otherwise: Race, Gender, and Implicit Understanding* (University Park: The Pennsylvania State University, 2011), 96.

34 Ibid., 190.

35 Ibid., 282.

36 Rachel Spronk, "Sexuality and Subjectivity: Erotic Practices and the Question of Bodily Sensations," *Social Anthropology* 22, no. 1 (2014): 3–21; Gordon Waitt, "Bodies that Sweat: The Affective Responses of Young Women in Wollongong, New South Wales, Australia," *Gender, Place and Culture* 21, no. 6 (2014): 666–82.

37 Fiona Newell and Ladan Shams, "New Insights into Multisensory Perception," *Perception* 36 (2007): 1415.

38 Maurice Merleau-Ponty, *Phenomenology of Perception*, trans. Colin Smith (London: Routledge & Kegan Paul, 1962).

39 Jan Slaby, "Affective Intentionality and the Feeling Body," *Phenomenology and the Cognitive Sciences* 7 (2008): 441.

40 George Lakoff and Mark Johnson, *Metaphors We Live By* (Chicago: University of Chicago, 1980); George Lakoff and Mark Johnson, *Philosophy in the Flesh: The Embodied Mind and Its Challenge to Western Thought* (New York: Basic Books, 1999).

41 See also, Benjamin Bergen, *Louder than Words: The New Science of How the Mind Makes Meaning* (New York: Basic Books, 2012).

42 Mark Johnson, *The Meaning of the Body: Aesthetics of Human Understanding* (Chicago: The University of Chicago, 2007).

43 See also Maxine Sheets-Johnstone, *The Primacy of Movement* (Philadelphia: John Benjamins Publishing Company, 1999).

44 Massumi, *Parables*, 95–96.

45 Jasbir K. Puar, *Terrorist Assemblages: Homonationalism in Queer Times* (Durham: Duke University, 2007); Jasbir K. Puar, "'I Would Rather Be a Cyborg than a Goddess': Becoming-Intersectional in Assemblage Theory," *philoSOPHIA* 2, no. 1 (2012): 49–66.

46 Merleau-Ponty, *Phenomenology of Perception*.

47 Michael Bull, Paul Gilroy, David Howes, and Douglas Kahn, "Introducing Sensory Studies," *The Senses and Society* 1 (2006): 5–7.

48 Howes, *Empire of the Senses*, 3.

49 Friedman, "Perceptual Construction," 82.

50 Howes and Classen, *Ways of Sensing*, 66; original emphasis.

51 Geurts, *Culture and the Senses*, 7–9.

52 Ibid., 3.

53 Pierre Bourdieu, *Outline of a Theory of Practice* (Cambridge: Cambridge University, 1977).

54 Karl Marx, *Economic and Philosophic Manuscripts of 1844*, trans. Martin Milligan (New York: International Publishers, 1964), 141.

55 Ibid., 139.

56 Ibid., 141.

57 Ibid., 143.

58 Ibid., 140–41; original emphasis.

59 Lee, "Asian Female Stereotypes," 89.

60 Saldanha, *Psychedelic White*, 8.

61 Richard Shusterman, *Body Consciousness: A Philosophy of Mindfulness and Somaesthetics* (Cambridge: Cambridge University, 2008), 25–26.

62 Saldanha, *Psychedelic White*.

Chapter 2

1 Gilles Deleuze and Félix Guattari, *A Thousand Plateaus: Capitalism and Schizophrenia*, trans. Brian Massumi (Minneapolis: University of Minnesota, 1987).

2 Jason Lim, "Immanent Politics: Thinking Race and Ethnicity through Affect and Machinism," *Environment and Planning A* 42 (2010): 2392–409, https://doi.org/doi:10.1068/a42234; Jasbir K. Puar, "'I Would Rather Be a Cyborg than a Goddess': Becoming-Intersectional in Assemblage Theory," *philoSOPHIA* 2, no. 1 (2012): 49–66; Arun Saldanha, "Reontologizing Race: The Machinic Geography of Phenotype," *Environment and Planning D: Society and Space* 24 (2006): 9–24.

3 Dan Swanton, "Sorting Bodies: Race, Affect, and Everyday Multiculture in a Mill Town in Northern England," *Environment and Planning A* 42 (2010): 2332–50, https://doi.org/ 10.1068/a42395.

4 Ibid., 2338.

5 Zeus Leonardo and Michalinos Zembylas, "Whiteness as Technology of Affect: Implications for Educational Praxis," *Equity and Excellence in Education* 46, no. 1 (2013): 158–59.

6 Ibid., 151.

7 Sara Ahmed, "Collective Feelings. Or, the Impressions Left by Others," *Theory, Culture & Society* 21, no. 2 (2004): 25–42.

8 Michalinos Zembylas, "Rethinking Race and Racism as *Technologies of Affect*: Theorizing the Implications for Anti-racist Politics and Practice in Education," *Race Ethnicity and Education* 18, no. 2 (2015): 148, https://doi.org/ 10.1080/13613324.2014.946492

9 Jasbir K. Puar, *Terrorist Assemblages: Homonationalism in Queer Times* (Durham: Duke University, 2007), 128.

10 Erin Manning, *Politics of Touch: Space, Movement, Sovereignty* (Minneapolis: University of Minnesota, 2007).

11 David Howes and Constance Classen, *Ways of Sensing: Understanding the Senses in Society* (New York: Routledge, 2014), 79; original emphasis.

12 Benedict Anderson, *Imagined Communities: Reflections on the Origin and Spread of Nationalism* (London: Verso, 1983).

13 Kathryn Linn Geurts, *Culture and the Senses: Bodily Ways of Knowing in an African Community* (Berkeley: University of California, 2002).

14 Howes and Classen, *Ways of Sensing*, 84.

15 Ahmed, "Collective Feelings."

16 Jennifer Lynn Stoever, *The Sonic Color Line: Race and the Cultural Politics of Listening* (New York: New York University, 2016).

17 Osagie K. Obasogie, "Do Blind People See Race? Social, Legal, and Theoretical Considerations," *Law & Society Review* 44, no. 3 (2010): 585–616.

18 Asia Friedman, "'There Are Two People at Work That I'm Fairly Certain Are Black': Uncertainty and Deliberative Thinking in Blind Race Attribution," *The Sociological Quarterly* 57 (2016): 437–61.

19 Ibid., 450, 456.

20 Martin Berger, *Sight Unseen: Whiteness and American Visual Culture* (Berkeley: University of California, 2005), 1; emphasis added.

21 Solomon Gustavo, "Inside Black Lives Matter: The Very Hard Job of Becoming the Traveling Church of Civil Rights," *City Pages*, July 27, 2016, http://www.citypages.com/news/inside-black-lives-matter-the-very-hard-job-of-becoming-the-traveling-church-of-civil-rights/388277802.

22 Friedman, "Blind Race Attribution," 438.

23 Constance Classen, *Worlds of Senses: Exploring the Senses in History and across Cultures* (New York: Routledge, 1993), 59.

24 Linda Alcoff argued that we must "make visible the practices of visibility itself, to outline the background from which our knowledge of others and of ourselves appears in relief. From there we may be able to alter the associated meanings ascribed to visible difference." *Visible Identities: Race, Gender, and the Self* (New York: Oxford University, 2006), 194.

25 Mark Smith, *How Race Is Made: Slavery, Segregation, and the Senses* (Chapel Hill: The University of North Carolina Press, 2006).

26 See Butler's discussion on the politics of racial visibility in Judith Butler, "Endangered/Endangering: Schematic Racism and White Paranoia," in *Reading Rodney King, Reading Urban Uprising*, ed. Robert Gooding-Williams (New York: Routledge, 1993), 15–22.

27 Ruth Frankenberg, "'When We Are Capable of Stopping, We Begin to See': Being White, Seeing Whiteness," in *Names We Call Home: Autobiography on Racial Identity*, ed. Becky Thompson and Sangeeta Tyagi (New York: Routledge, 1996), 14.

28 Elaine Scarry, *The Body in Pain: The Making and Unmaking of the World* (New York: Oxford University, 1985), 13.

29 Ibid., 12.

30 Ibid., 14.

31 David Morris, *The Culture of Pain* (Los Angeles: University of California, 1991), 3.

32 Constance Classen, ed., *The Book of Touch* (New York: Berg, 2005), 110.

33 Smith, *How Race Is Made.*

34 Ibid., 4.

35 Ibid., 4, 64.

36 Ibid., 7.

37 Howes, *Empire of the Senses*, 10.

38 Smith, *How Race Is Made.*

39 Morris, *The Culture of Pain*, 39.

40 Shannon Sullivan addressed white privilege as psychosomatic habits. *Revealing Whiteness: The Unconscious Habits of Racial Privilege* (Bloomington: Indiana University, 2004).

41 Smith, *How Race Is Made*, 48.

42 bell hooks, *Black Looks: Race and Representation* (Boston: South End Press, 1992), 168.

43 Various empirical studies suggest that individuals' sensory perception of others' pain is racialized. See, for example, Alessio Avenanti, Angela Sirigu, and Salvatore M. Aglioti, "Racial Bias Reduces Empathic Sensorimotor Resonance with Other-Race Pain," *Current Biology* 20 (2010): 1018–22; Xu, Xiangyu Zuo Xiaojing, Xiaoying Wang, and Shihui Han, "Do You Feel My Pain? Racial Group Membership Modulates Empathic Neural Responses," *The Journal of Neuroscience* 29 (2009): 8525–29.

44 David E. Sutton, "Food and the Senses," *Annual Review of Anthropology* 39 (2010): 211.

45 Rachel Spronk and Christian Klaufus, "Introduction: Taste," *Etnofoor* 24, no. 2 (2012): 9.

46 Ashis Nandy, "Ethnic Cuisine: The Significant 'Other,'" *India International Centre Quarterly* 9, no. 3 (2003): 248.

47 hooks, *Black Looks*, 21–39.

48 Alex Rhys-Taylor, "Disgust and Distinction: The Case of the Jellied Eel," *The Sociological Review* 61 (2013): 227–46.

49 Camille Bégin, *Taste of the Nation: The New Deal Search for America's Food* (Urbana: University of Illinois Press, 2016), 85.

50 Ibid., 88.

51 Ibid.

52 Robert Ji-Song Ku, *Dubious Gastronomy: The Cultural Politics of Eating Asian in the USA* (Honolulu: University of Hawaii, 2014), 13.

53 Ibid.

54 Kelvin E. Y. Low, *Scent and Scent-sibilities: Smell and Everyday Life Experiences* (Newcastle-upon-Tyne: Cambridge Scholars Publishing, 2009), 14.

55 Constance Classen, "The Odor of the Other: Olfactory Symbolism and Cultural Categories," *Ethos* 20, no. 2 (1992): 133–66; Constance Classen, David Howes, and Anthony Synnott, *Aroma: The Cultural History of Smell* (London and New York: Routledge, 1994); Kevin E. Y. Low, "Olfactive Frames of Remembering: Theorizing Self, Senses and Society," *The Sociological Review* 61 (2013): 688–708; Sarah Pink, *Doing Sensory Ethnography* (Los Angeles: Sage, 2009); Dennis Waskul, Phillip Vannini, and Janelle Wilson, "The Aroma of Recollection: Olfaction, Nostalgia, and the Shaping of the Sensuous Self," *The Senses and Society* 4, no. 1 (2009): 5–22, https://doi.org/10.2752/174589309X388546; Amanda Wise and Adam Chapman, "Introduction: Migration, Affect, and the Senses," *Journal of Intercultural Studies* 26, no. 1–2 (2005): 1–3.

56 Anthony Synnott, "Puzzling Over the Senses: From Plato to Marx," in *The Varieties of Sensory Experience. A Source Book in the Anthropology of the Senses,* ed. David Howes (Toronto: University of Toronto, 1991), 71–76.

57 Gale Peter Largey and David Rodney Watson, "The Sociology of Odors," *American Journal of Sociology* 77, no. 6 (1972): 1024, https://www.jstor.org/stable/2776218.

58 Classen et al., *Aroma*, 173.

59 Classen, "The Odor of the Other," 135.

60 Martin F. Manalansan IV, "Immigrant Lives and the Politics of Olfaction in the Global City," in *The Smell Culture Reader*, ed. Jim Drobnick (Oxford: Berg, 2006), 41–52.

61 Low, *Scent and Scent-sibilities*.

62 Ibid., 86.

63 Michelle Ferranti, "An Odor of Racism: Vaginal Deodorants in African-American Beauty Culture and Advertising," *Advertising & Society Review* 11, no. 4 (2011), https://muse.jhu.edu/.

64 Ferranti, "An Odor of Racism."

65 Stoever, *The Sonic Color Line*.

66 Ibid., 29–31.

67 Ibid., 36–42.

68 Ian Haney López, *Dog Whistle Politics: How Coded Racial Appeals Have Reinvented Racism and Wrecked the Middle Class* (New York: Oxford University, 2014).

69   Christopher Brown, "Book Review: *Dog Whistle Politics: How Coded Racial Appeals Have Reinvented Racism and Wrecked the Middle Class*," *Journalism and Mass Communication Quarterly* 92, no. 4 (2015): 1011.

70   López, *Dog Whistle Politics*, 142.

71   Jennifer Lynn Stoever, "Fine-tuning the Sonic Color-line: Radio and the Acousmatic Du Bois," *Modernist Cultures* 10, no. 1 (2015): 99–118.

72   Ibid., 101–5.

73   Geoff Mann, "Why Does Country Music Sound White? Race and the Voice of Nostalgia," *Ethnic and Racial Studies* 31, no. 1 (2008): 73–100.

74   Ibid., 74.

75   Ibid., 92.

76   Puar, *Terrorist Assemblages*.

77   Howes and Classen, *Ways of Sensing*.

78   Arun Saldanha, *Psychedelic White: Goa Trance and the Viscosity of Race* (Minneapolis: University of Minnesota, 2007), 50.

79   Ibid., 206.

80   Ibid., 207.

Chapter 3

1   Emily S. Lee, *Living Alterities: Phenomenology, Embodiment, and Race* (Albany: SUNY Press, 2014), 7.

2   Sachi Sekimoto, "A Multimodal Approach to Identity: Theorizing the Self through Embodiment, Spatiality, and Temporality," *Journal of International and Intercultural Communication* 5, no. 3 (2012): 227, http://dx.doi.org/10.1080/17513057.2012.689314.

3   Sachi Sekimoto, "Transnational Asia: Dis/orienting Identity in the Globalized World," *Communication Quarterly* 62, no. 4 (2014): 381–98, http://dx.doi.org/10.1080/014633 73.2014.922485.

4   Leo Ching, "Globalizing the Regional, Regionalizing the Global: Mass Culture and Asianism in the Age of Late Capital," *Public Culture* 12, no. 1 (2000): 233–57.

5   Koichi, Iwabuchi, "Complicit Exoticism: Japan and Its Other," *Continuum* 8, no. 2 (1994): 49–82; Ge Sun, "How Does Asia Mean? (Part I)," *Inter-Asia Cultural Studies* 1, no. 1 (2000): 13–47; Ge Sun, "How Does Asia Mean? (Part II)," *Inter-Asia Cultural Studies* 1, no. 2 (2000): 319–41; Yiman Wang, "Screening Asia: Passing, Performative Translation, and Reconfiguration," *Positions* 15, no. 2 (2007): 319–43.

6   Frantz Fanon, *Black Skin, White Masks*, trans. Charles Lam Markmann (New York: Grove, 1967), 109.

7   Emily S. Lee, "The Epistemology of the Question of Authenticity, in Place of Strategic Essentialism," *Hypatia: A Journal of Feminist Philosophy* 26, no. 2 (2011): 263.

8   Alia Al-Saji, "A Phenomenology of Hesitation: Interrupting Racializing Habits of Seeing," in *Living Alterities: Phenomenology, Embodiment, and Race*, ed. Emily S. Lee (Albany: SUNY Press, 2014), 138.

9   Kyoo Lee, "Why Asian Female Stereotypes Matter to All: Beyond Black and White, East and West," *Critical Philosophy of Race* 1, no. 1 (2013): 98.

10 Laura U. Marks, *The Skin of the Film: Intercultural Cinema, Embodiment, and the Senses* (Durham: Duke University Press, 2000).

11 Daniel Black, "What Is a Face?" *Body & Society* 17, no. 4 (2011): 2, https://doi.org/10.1177/1357034X11410450.

12 Beata Stawarska, "Mutual Gaze and Social Cognition," *Phenomenology and the Cognitive Sciences* 5 (2006): 23, https://doi.org/10.1007/s11097-005-9009-4.

13 Beata Stawarska, "Seeing Faces: Sartre and Imitation Studies," *Sartre Studies International* 13, no. 2 (2007): 28–29, https://doi.org/10.3167/ssi.2007/130202.

14 Jonathan Cole, "Empathy Needs a Face," *Journal of Consciousness Studies* 8, no. 5–7 (2001): 51–68.

15 Ibid., 55.

16 David Le Breton, "From Disfigurement to Facial Transplant: Identity Insights," *Body & Society* 21, no. 4 (2015): 6, https://doi.org/10.1177/1357034X14536448.

17 Maurice Merleau-Ponty, *Phenomenology of Perception*, trans. Colin Smith (London: Routledge & Kegan Paul, 1962), 146.

18 Jon D. Rutter, "Dismantling the Face: Toward a Phenomenology of Boxing," *Cultural Studies ↔ Critical Methodologies* 7, no. 3 (2007): 285, https://doi.org/10.1177/1532708606297159.

19 Ruth Ozeki, *The Face: A Time Code* (Brooklyn: Restless Books, 2015), 129.

20 Ibid., 12.

21 Chris Abani, *The Face: Cartography of the Void* (Brooklyn: Restless Books, 2013), 84.

22 Stawarska, "Mutual Gaze," 17–18.

23 Stawarska, "Seeing Face," 29–32.

24 Kiyokazu Washida, 鷲田清一, *Kao no Genshōgaku* 顔の現象学 [Phenomenology of the Face] (Tokyo: Kōdansha, 1996), 196.

25 Stawarska, "Seeing Faces," 34.

26 Florentina C. Andreescu, "Face and Facial Disfigurations: Self and Alterations of Self," *Psychotherapy and Politics International* 15, no. 2 (2017): 7, https://doi.org/10.1002/ppi.1407.

27 Rachel Alicia Griffin, "Pushing Precious: Black Women, Media Representation, and the Glare of the White Supremacist Capitalist Patriarchal Gaze," *Critical Studies in Media Communication* 31, no. 3 (2014): 182–97, https://doi.org/10.1080/15295036.2013.849354; bell hooks, *Black Looks: Race and Representation* (Boston: South End Press, 1992), 115–31.

28 Sara Ahmed, "A Phenomenology of Whiteness." *Feminist Theory* 8 (2007): 149–68.

29 Gilles Deleuze and Félix Guattari, *A Thousand Plateaus: Capitalism and Schizophrenia*, trans. Brian Massumi (Minneapolis: University of Minnesota, 1987), 178.

30 David Haekwon Kim, "Shame and Self-Revision in Asian American Assimilation," in *Living Alterities: Phenomenology, Embodiment, and Race*, ed. Emily S. Lee (Albany: SUNY Press, 2014), 199.

31 Helen Ngo, *The Habits of Racism: A Phenomenology of Racism and Racialized Embodiment* (Lanham: Lexington Books, 2017), 143.

32 Le Breton, "Disfigurement," 9.

33 Marks, *The Skin of the Film*, 162.

34 Ibid., 162–63.

35 Shannon Sullivan, "The Hearts and Guts of White People: Ethics, Ignorance, and the Physiology of White Racism," *Journal of Religious Ethics* 42, no. 4 (2014): 591–611.

36 David Le Breton, *Sensing the World: An Anthropology of the Senses*, trans. Carmen Ruschiensky (London: Bloomsbury Academic, 2017), ch. 2, Kindle.

37 Fanon, *Black Skin, White Masks*, 112.

38 Ahmed, "Whiteness," 161.

39 Sara Ahmed and Jackie Stacey, *Thinking Through the Skin* (New York: Routledge, 2001).

40 Marc Lafrance, "Skin and the Self: Cultural Theory and Anglo-American Psychoanalysis," *Body & Society* 15, no. 3 (2009): 8, https://doi.org/10.1177/1357034X09339099.

41 David Howes, "The Skinscape: Reflections on the Dermalogical Turn," *Body & Society* 24, no. 1–2 (2018): 229, https://doi.org/10.1177/1357034X18766285.

42 Erin Manning, *Politics of Touch: Space, Movement, Sovereignty* (Minneapolis: University of Minnesota Press, 2007).

43 Ibid., introduction, Kindle.

44 David Howes, ed., "Introduction," in *Empire of the Senses: The Sensual Culture Reader* (Oxford: Berg, 2005), 7.

45 Ahmed, "Whiteness," 163.

46 Sara Ahmed, "Home and Away: Narratives of Migration and Estrangement," *International Journal of Cultural Studies* 2, no. 3 (1999), 341.

47 Ibid.

48 Ahmed, "Whiteness," 158; original emphasis.

49 George Yancy, *Look, a White!: Philosophical Essays on Whiteness* (Philadelphia: Temple University Press, 2012), 45.

50 Ahmed, "Whiteness," 161.

51 Massumi, *Parables*, 2–4.

Chapter 4

1 Elizabeth Behnke, "Interkinaesthetic Affectivity: A Phenomenological Approach," *Continental Philosophy* 41, no. 2 (2008): 145.

2 Katrín Lund, "Seeing in Motion and the Touching Eye: Walking over Scotland's Mountain," *Etnofoor* 18, no. 1 (2005): 30.

3 Behnke, "Interkinaesthetic Affectivity," 147.

4 Rod Brunson, "Police Don't Like Black People: African-American Young Men's Accumulated Police Experiences," *Criminology and Public Policy* 6, no. 1 (2007): 71–102; William Terrill and Michael Reisig, "Neighborhood Context and Police Use of Force," *Journal of Research on Crime and Delinquency* 40, no. 3 (2003): 291–321.

5 Malcolm D. Holmes and Brad W. Smith, *Race and Police Brutality: Roots of an Urban Dilemma* (Albany: SUNY Press, 2008); David S. Kirk and Andrew V. Papachristos, "Cultural Mechanisms and the Persistence of Neighborhood," *American Journal of Sociology* 11, no. 4 (2011): 1190–233.

6 Michal Pagis, "Embodied Self-reflexivity," *Social Psychology Quarterly* 72 (2009): 265–83.

7 Maurice Merleau-Ponty, *Phenomeology of Perception*, trans. Colin Smith (London: Routledge and Kegan Paul, 1962).

8 Simone de Beauvoir, *The Second Sex*, trans. Constance Borde and Sheila Malovany-Chevallier (New York: Alfred A. Knope, 2010), 46.

9 Sara Ahmed, "A Phenomenology of Whiteness," *Feminist Theory* 8, no. 2 (2008): 161.

10 Frantz Fanon, *Black Skins, White Masks*, trans. Richard Philcox (New York: Grove Press, 2008), 95.

11 Lisa Hunter and Elke Emerald, "Sensory Narratives: Capturing Embodiment in Narratives of Movement, Sport, Leisure, and Health," *Sport, Education, and Society* 21, no. 1 (2016): 32.

12 Behnke, "Interkinaesthetic Affectivity," 146.

13 Ibid., 148.

14 Rosalyn Diprose, *Corporeal Generosity: On Giving with Nietzsche, Merleau-Ponty and Levinas* (Albany: State University of New York Press, 2002).

15 Tomoko Tamari, "The Phenomenology of Architecture: A Short Introduction to Juhani Pallasmaa," *Body & Society* 23, no. 1 (2017): 93.

16 George Yancy, *Black Bodies, White Gazes: The Continuing Significance of Race* (Lanham: Rowman and Littlefield, 2008).

17 Ibid., 4.

18 Fanon, *Black Skins, White Masks*, 92

19 Coates takes this title from a Richard Wright poem that narrates the hardships and pain of lynching experienced by Negro Americans during the eras of slavery and separate but equal in the United States.

20 Ta-Nehisi Coates, *Between the World and Me* (New York: Spiegel & Grau, 2015), 12.

21 Ibid., 71.

22 Fanon, *Black Skins, White Masks*, 95

23 Linda Martín Alcoff, *Visible Identities: Race, Gender and the Self* (Oxford: Oxford University Press, 2006); Maurice Merleau-Ponty, *Phenomenology of Perception*, trans. Colin Smith (London: Routledge and Kegan Paul, 1962).

24 Coates, *Between the World and Me*, 12.

25 Ibid., 111.

26 Ibid., 8.

27 Ibid., 103.

28 Constance Classen, *Worlds of Sense: Exploring the Senses in History and Across Cultures* (New York: Routledge, 1993); Mark M. Smith, *How Race Is Made: Slavery, Segregation, and the Senses* (Chapel Hill: University of North Carolina Press, 2006).

29 Brunson, "Police Don't Like Black People," 81–92; Joe Feagin, "The Continuing Significance of Race: Anti-black Discrimination in Public Places," *Sociological Review* 56, no. 1 (1991): 101–16; Dennis P. Rosenbaum, Amie M. Schuck, Sandra K. Costello, Darnell F. Hawkins, and Marianne K. Ring, "Attitudes toward the Police: The Effects of Direct and Vicarious Experience," *Police Quarterly* 8, no. 3 (2005): 343–65; Tom R. Tyler and Cheryl J. Wakslak, "Profiling and Police Legitimacy: Procedural Justice, Attributions of Motive, and Acceptance of Police Authority," *Criminology* 42, no. 2 (2004): 253–82; Ronald Weitzer, "Racialized Policing: Residents' Perceptions in Three Neighborhoods," *Law & Society Review* 34, no. 1 (2000): 129–55.

Chapter 5

1   John L. Austin, *How to Do Things with Words: The William James Lectures Delivered in Harvard University in 1955*, ed. James Opie Urmson and Marina Sbisá (Cambridge: Harvard University Press, 1962).

2   Judith Butler, *Bodies that Matter: On the Discursive Limits of "Sex"* (New York: Routledge, 1993).

3   Pierre Bourdieu, *Outline of a Theory of Practice*, trans. Richard Nice (Cambridge: Cambridge University Press, 1977); Maurice Merleau-Ponty, *Phenomenology of Perception*, trans. Colin Smith (New York: Routledge & Kegan Paul, 1962).

4   Ibid.

5   Homi K. Bhabha, *The Location of Culture* (New York: Routledge, 1994), 121–31.

6   For a discussion on the relationship between language and kinesthetic understanding of reality, see Sachiko Tankei-Aminian, "On Becoming Japersican: A Personal Narrative of Cultural Adaptation, Intercultural Identity, and Transnationalism," in *Globalizing Intercultural Communication: A Reader*, ed. Kathryn Sorrells and Sachi Sekimoto (Thousand Oaks: Sage, 2016), 198–99.

7   Martin Heidegger, *Being and Time*, trans. John Macquarrie and Edward Robinson (New York: Harper and Row, 1962).

8   Adesola Akinleye, "Orientation for Communication: Embodiment, and the Language of Dance," *Empedocles: European Journal for the Philosophy of Communication* 4, no. 2 (2013): 101–12; Bryant K. Alexander and John T. Warren, "The Materiality of Bodies: Critical Reflections on Pedagogy, Politics and Positionality," *Communication Quarterly* 50, no. 3–4 (2002): 328–43; Leslie Maria Bowen, "Reconfigured Bodies: The Problem of Ownership," *Communication Theory* 15, no. 1 (2005): 23–38; Devika Chawla and Amardo Rodriguez, "Postcoloniality and the Speaking Body: Revisioning the English Oral Competency Curriculum," *Cultural Studies ←→ Critical Methodologies* 11, no. 1 (2011): 76–91; Megan Foley, "'Prove You're Human': Fetishizing Material Embodiment and Immaterial Labor in Information Networks," *Critical Studies in Media Communication* 31, no. 5 (2014): 365–79; Wendelin M. Küpers, "'Intercommunicating': Phenomenological Perspectives on Embodied Communication and Contextuality," *Journal for Communication & Culture* 2, no. 2 (2012): 114–38; Claudio Moreira and Marcelo Diversi, "Missing Bodies: Troubling the Colonial Landscape of American Academia," *Text and Performance Quarterly* 31, no. 3 (2011): 229–48; Julie-Ann Scott, "Stories of Hyperembodiment: An Analysis of Personal Narratives of and through Physically Disabled Bodies," *Text and Performance Quarterly* 32, no. 2 (2012): 100–20; Sachi Sekimoto, "A Multimodal Approach to Identity: Theorizing the Self through Embodiment, Spatiality, and Temporality," *Journal of International and Intercultural Communication* 5, no. 3 (2012): 226–43.

9   John T. Warren and Amy K. Kilgard, "Staging Stain upon the Snow: Performance as a Critical Enfleshment of Whiteness," *Text and Performance Quarterly* 21, no. 4 (2001): 263–76.

10 Alexander and Warren, "The Materiality of Bodies," 341; Peter McLaren, *Schooling as a Ritual Performance: Towards a Political Economy of Education Symbols and Gestures* (New York: Routledge, 1986).

11 Gust A. Yep, "Queering/Quaring/Kauering/Crippin'/Transing 'Other Bodies' in Intercultural Communication," *Journal of International and Intercultural Communication* 6, no. 2 (2013): 123.

12 Scott, "Stories of Hyperembodiment."

13 Moreira and Diversi, "Missing Bodies."

14 Sara Ahmed, *On Being Included: Racism and Diversity in Institutional Life* (Durham: Duke University Press, 2012), 129; original emphasis.

15 Merleau-Ponty, *Phenomenology of Perception*, 211.

16 Bourdieu, *Outline of a Theory of Practice*, 87.

17 Ibid., 78.

18 Bhabha, *The Location of Culture*, 126; original emphasis.

19 Ibid.

20 Liam Grealy, "Negotiating Cultural Authenticity in Hip-Hop: Mimicry, Whiteness and Eminem," *Continuum: Journal of Media & Cultural Studies* 22, no. 6 (2008): 857.

21 bell hooks, *Teaching to Transgress: Education as the Practice of Freedom* (New York: Routledge, 1994), 167–76.

22 Felicia R. Lee, "Lingering Conflict in the Schools: Black Dialect vs. Standard Speech," *The New York Times*, January 5, 1994, accessed April 11, 2015, http://www.nytimes.com/1994/01/05/nyregion/lingering-conflict-in-the-schools-black-dialectvs-standard-speech.html?pagewanted=all.

23 Marwan M. Kraidy, "Hybridity in Cultural Globalization," *Communication Theory* 12, no. 3 (2002): 316–39.

24 Merleau-Ponty, *Phenomenology of Perception*; Shaun Gallagher and Dan Zahavi, *The Phenomenological Mind: An Introduction to Philosophy of Mind and Cognitive Science* (New York: Routledge, 2008); Thomas Nagel, "What Is It Like to Be a Bat?" *The Philosophical Review* 83, no. 4 (1974): 435–50.

25 Sara Ahmed, "A Phenomenology of Whiteness," *Feminist Theory* 8, no. 2 (2007): 149–68; Jacqueline M. Martinez, *Phenomenology of Chicana Experience and Identity: Communication and Transformation in Praxis* (Lanham: Rowman & Littlefield, 2000); Nagel, "What Is It Like to Be a Bat?"

26 Arthur P. Bochner, "On First-Person Narrative Scholarship: Autoethnography as Acts of Meaning," *Narrative Inquiry* 22, no. 1 (2012): 155–64; Carolyn Ellis, *Revision: Autoethnographic Reflections on Life and Work* (Walnut Creek: Left Coast Press, 2009); Stacy Holman Jones, "Autoethnography: Making the Personal Political," in *Handbook of Qualitative Research*, ed. Norman K. Denzin and Yvonna S. Lincoln (Thousand Oaks: Sage, 2005), 763–91.

27 Sachi Sekimoto, "Transnational Asia: Dis/orienting Identity in the Globalized World," *Communication Quarterly* 62, no. 4 (2014): 387.

28 Austin, *How to Do Things with Words.*

29 Donaldo Macedo, Bessie Dendrinos, and Panayota Gounari, *The Hegemony of English* (Boulder: Paradigm, 2003); Yukio Tsuda, "Speaking against the Hegemony of English: Problems, Ideologies, and Solutions," in *The Handbook of Critical Intercultural Communication*, ed. Thomas K. Nakayama and Rona Tamiko Halualani (Malden: Wiley-Blackwell, 2010), 248–69.

30 Bourdieu, *Outline of a Theory of Practice*, 78–95.

31 Chawla and Rodriguez, "Postcoloniality and the Speaking Body," 80.

32 Merleau-Ponty, *Phenomenology of Perception.*

33 Pensri Ho, "Performing the 'Oriental': Professionals and the Asian Model Minority Myth," *Journal of Asian American Studies* 6, no. 2 (2003): 149–75; Yuko Kawai, "Stereotyping Asian Americans: The Dialectic of the Model Minority and the Yellow Peril," *Howard Journal of Communications* 16, no. 2 (2005): 109–30.

34 H. Samy Alim and Geneva Smitherman, *Articulate while Black: Barak Obama, Language, and Race in the US* (Oxford: Oxford University Press, 2012).

35 John McWhorter, "The Perpetual Failure to Understand Obama's Double Consciousness," *New Republic*, October 3, 2012, accessed January 13, 2015, http://www.newrepublic.com/article/108180/perpetual-failure-understand-obamasdouble-consciousness.

36 James Baldwin, "If Black English Isn't a Language, then Tell Me, What Is?" *The New York Times*, July 29, 1979, accessed January 13, 2015, https://www.nytimes.com/books/98/03/29/specials/baldwin-english.html; Henry Louis Gates, *The Signifying Monkey: A Theory of African American Literary Criticism* (Oxford: Oxford University Press, 1988).

37 Merleau-Ponty, *Phenomenology of Perception*, 195.

38 Ibid., 192.

39 Ibid., 392; original emphasis.

40 Frantz Fanon, quoted in Linda Martín Alcoff, *Visible Identities: Race, Gender, and the Self* (Oxford: Oxford University Press, 2006), 187.

41 Merleau-Ponty, *Phenomenology of Perception.*

42 Baldwin, "If Black English Isn't a Language"; Gates, *The Signifying Monkey*; Geneva Smitherman, *Talkin and Testifyin: The Language of Black America* (Boston: Houghton Mifflin, 1977).

43 Michael J. Beatty, James McCroskey, and Kory Floyd, eds., *Biological Dimensions of Communication: Perspectives, Research, and Methods* (Creskill: Hampton, 2009); William J. Hardcastle, John Laver, and Fiona E. Gibbon, eds., *The Handbook of Phonetic Sciences*, 2nd ed. (Malden: Wiley-Blackwell, 2013).

44 Hans Ulrich Gumbrecht and K. Ludwig Pfeiffer, eds., *Materialities of Communication*, trans. William Whobrey (Stanford: Stanford University Press, 1994); Friedrich A. Kittler, *Discourse Networks 1800/1900*, trans. Michael Metteer and Chris Cullens (Stanford: Stanford University Press, 1990); Timothy Kuhn, ed., *Matters of Communication: Political, Cultural and Technological Challenges* (New York: Hampton Press, 2011); Marshall McLuhan, *Understanding Media: The Extensions of Man* (New York: McGraw-Hill, 1964).

45 Annette Schlichter, "Do Voices Matter? Vocality, Materiality, Gender Performativity," *Body & Society* 17, no. 1 (2011): 31–52; Veronica Vasterling, "Body and Language: Butler, Merleau-Ponty and Lyotard on the Speaking Embodied Subject," *International Journal of Philosophical Studies* 11, no. 2 (2003): 205–23.

46 Judith Butler, "Performative Acts and Gender Constitution: An Essay in Phenomenology and Feminist Theory," *Theatre Journal* 40, no. 4 (1988): 525.

47 Butler, *Bodies that Matter*, 30.

48 Iris Marion Young, *On Female Body Experience: "Throwing Like a Girl" and Other Essays* (New York: Oxford University, 2005), 27–45.

Chapter 6

1 Christopher Brown, "Black like Me, Black like I Am! Language and Memories of Race in Higher Education," in *Globalizing Intercultural Communication: A Reader*, ed. Kathryn Sorrells and Sachi Sekimoto (Los Angeles: Sage, 2016), 117.

2 Peter R. Breggin, "Empathic Self-Transformation and Love in Individual and Family Therapy," *Humanistic Psychologist* 27, no. 3 (1999): 267–82. Carl Rogers, "Empathic: An Unappreciated Way of Being," *Counseling Psychologist* 5, no. 2 (1975): 2–10. Edith Stein, *On the Problem of Empathy*, trans. Waltraut Stein (Washington DC: Institute of Carmelite Studies Publications, 1989).

3 Stein, *On the Problem of Empathy*, 6.

4 Ibid., 14.

5 Rogers, "Empathic: An Unappreciated Way of Being," 5.

6 Breggin, "Empathic Self-Transformation," 270.

7 Peter Rosan, "The Poetics of Intersubjective Life: Empathy and the Other," *Humanistic Psychologist* 40, no. 2 (2012): 115–36.

8 Stein, *On the Problem of Empathy*, 11.

9 Maurice Merleau-Ponty, *Phenomenology of Perception*, trans. Colin Smith (London: Routledge & Kegan Paul, 1945/1962), 185.

10 I defined white male elites as those who self-identified as white, work in high-profile positions such as chief executive officer and president. These men occupy spaces

in which they can reside in various privileged locations: white, male, nominally heterosexual, affluent relative to economic status, and privileged relative to education status. Unlike people of color and white women, institutional spaces are organized around white male elites' rhetorical faculties, linguistic styles, and cultural repertoires.

11   Christopher Brown, "Barack Obama as the Great Man: Communicative Constructions of Racial Transcendence in White-Male Elite Discourses," *Communication Monographs* 78, no. 4 (2011): 535–56.

12   For exceptions see the work of Brown, "Barack Obama as the Great Man," 541–50; Joe R. Feagin and Eileen O'Brien, *White Men on Race: Power, Privilege, and the Shaping of a Cultural Consciousness* (Beacon: Beacon Press, 2003).

13   Eduardo Bonilla-Silva and Tyrone A. Forman, "'I am Not Racist but': Mapping White College Students' Racial Ideology in the USA," *Discourse and Society*, 11 (2000): 50–85. Ronald L. Jackson and Susan M. Heckman, "Perceptions of White Identity and White Liability: An Analysis of White Student Responses to a College Campus Racial Hate Crime," *Journal of Communication* 52, no. 2 (2002): 434–50; Judith N. Martin, Robert L. Krizek, Thomas L. Nakayama, and Lisa Bradford, "What Do White People Want to be called? A Study of Self-Labels for White Americans," in *Whiteness: The Communication of Social Identity*, ed. Judith N. Martin, Robert L. Krizek, Thomas L. Nakayama, and Lisa Bradford (Thousand Oaks: Sage, 1996), 27–50; Dreama Moon, "White Enculturation and Bourgeois Ideology: The Discursive Production of Good White Girls," in *Whiteness: The Communication of Social Identity*, ed. Judith N. Martin, Robert L. Krizek, Thomas L. Nakayama, and Lisa Bradford (Thousand Oaks: Sage, 1996), 177–97; Pamela Perry, "White Universal Identity as a 'Sense of Group Position,'" *Symbolic Interaction* 30, no. 3 (2007): 375–93.

14   Kristen A Myers and Passion Williamson, "Race Talk: The Perpetuation of Racism through Private Discourse," *Race and Society* 4, no. 1 (2001): 3–26.

15   Eduardo Bonilla-Silva, Amanda Lewis, and David G. Embrick, "'I Did Not Get that Job because a Black Man . . .' The Story Lines and Testimonies of Colorblind Racism," *Sociological Forum* 19, no. 4 (2004): 555–81; Joe Feagin, *The White Racial Frame: Centuries of Racial Framing and Counter-Framing* (New York: Routledge, 2010).

16   Linda M. Alcoff, *Visible Identities: Race, Gender, and the Self* (New York: Oxford University Press, 2006), 179.

17   Kristen M. Langellier and Eric E. Peterson, *Performative Narrative: The Storytelling in Daily Life* (Philadelphia: Temple University Press, 2011), 164.

18   Ruth Frankenberg, *White Women, Race Matters: The Social Construction of Whiteness* (Minneapolis: University of Minnesota, 1993).

19   George Lipsitz, *The Possessive Investment in Whiteness: How White People Profit from Identity Politics* (Philadelphia: Temple University Press, 2006), 4–5.

20   Robyn Wiegman, "Whiteness Studies and the Paradox of Particularity," *Boundary* 26, no. 3 (1999): 115–50.

21   Robin DeAngelo, *White Fragility: Why Is It So Hard for White People to Talk about Racism* (Boston: Beacon Press, 2018), 15.

22 Charles Mills, *The Racial Contract* (Ithaca: Cornell University Press, 1997), 53.

23 Erving Goffman, *The Presentation of Self in Everyday Life* (London: Penguin Press, 1990).

24 Sara Ahmed, "A Phenomenology of Whiteness," *Feminist Theory* 8, no. 2 (2008): 153.

25 Bonilla-Silva, Lewis, and Embrick, "I Did Not Get that Job because a Black Man . . . ," 571.

26 Frankenberg, *White Women, Race Matters*, 149.

27 Breggin, "Empathic Self-Transformation," 269.

28 Reni Eddo-Lodge, *Why I'm No Longer Talking to White People about Race* (London: Bloomsbury, 2017).

Chapter 7

1 Shannon Sullivan, "The Hearts and Guts of White People: Ethics, Ignorance, and the Physiology of White Racism," *Journal of Religious Ethics* 42, no. 4 (2014): 592, original emphasis.

2 Ibid.

3 David A. Granger, "Somaesthetics and Racism: Toward an Embodied Pedagogy of Difference," *Journal of Aesthetic Education* 44, no. 3 (2010): 69–81; Helen Ngo, *The Habits of Racism: A Phenomenology of Racism and Racialized Embodiment* (Lanham: Lexington Books, 2012); Shannon Sullivan, *The Physiology of Sexist and Racist Oppression* (Oxford: Oxford University, 2015).

4 Ibid., 592.

5 Martin Berger, *Sight Unseen: Whiteness and American Visual Culture* (Berkeley: University of California, 2005), 1.

6 Robin DiAngelo, *White Fragility: Why It's So Hard For White People to Talk About Racism* (Boston: Beacon Press, 2018).

7 Peggy McIntosh, "White Privilege: Unpacking the Invisible Knapsack," in *Race, Class, and Gender in the United States, 6th Edition: An Integrated Study*, ed. Paula Rothenberg (New York: Worth Publishers, 2004), 188–92; Charles Mills, *The Racial Contract* (Ithaca: Cornell University Press, 1997); Tim Wise, *White like Me: Reflections on Race from a Privileged Son* (Brooklyn: Soft Skull, 2008); George Yancy, *Black Bodies, White Gazes: The Continuing Significance of Race in America*, 2nd ed. (New York: Roman & Littlefield, 2017).

8 Ta-Nehisi Coates, *Between the World and Me* (New York: Spiegel & Grau, 2015), 10.

9 For a discussion on the senses as prosthetic devices, see Erin Manning, *Politics of Touch: Space, Movement, Sovereignty* (Minneapolis: University of Minnesota, 2007).

10 Arun Saldanha, "Reontologizing Race: The Machinic Geography of Phenotype," *Environment and Planning D: Society and Space* 24 (2006), 19.

11   Ibid., 18.

12   Ibid., 10.

13   Ibid.

14   Granger, "Somaesthetics," 78.

15   Richard Shusterman, "Somaesthetics and the Body/Media Issue," *Body & Society* 3, no. 3 (1997): 36.

16   Helen Ngo, "Racist Habits: A Phenomenological Analysis of Racism and the Habitual Body," *Philosophy and Social Criticism* 42, no. 9 (2016): 848.

17   Arun Saldanha, *Psychedelic White: Goa Trance and the Viscosity of Race* (Minneapolis: University of Minnesota, 2007).

18   Alia Al-Saji, "A Phenomenology of Hesitation: Interrupting Racializing Habits of Seeing," in *Living Alterities: Phenomenology, Embodiment, and Race*, ed. Emily S. Lee (Albany: SUNY Press, 2014), 133–72.

19   Ibid., 144–45.

20   Ngo, "Racist Habits."

21   Gail Weiss, "Sedimented Attitudes and Existential Responsibilities," in *Body/Self/Other: The Phenomenology of Social Encounters*, ed. Luna Dolezal and Danielle Petherbridge (Albany: SUNY Press, 2017), 75–102.

22   Danielle Petherbridge, "Racializing Perception and the Phenomenology of Invisibility," in *Body/Self/Other: The Phenomenology of Social Encounters*, ed. Luna Dolezal and Danielle Petherbridge (Albany: SUNY Press, 2017), 103–29.

23   David Howes, "Introduction: 'Make It New!'—Reforming the Sensory World," in *A Cultural History of the Senses in the Modern Age*, ed. David Howes (London: Bloomsbury, 2014), 20.

24   Danielle Petherbridge, "Racializing Perception and the Phenomenology of Invisibility," in *Body/Self/Other: The Phenomenology of Social Encounters*, ed. Luna Dolezal and Danielle Petherbridge (Albany: SUNY Press, 2017), 116.

25   Richard Shusterman, *Body Consciousness: A Philosophy of Mindfulness and Somaesthetics* (Cambridge: Cambridge University: 2008), 22.

26   Ibid., 25–26.

27   Weiss, "Sedimented Attitudes," 86.

28   Granger, "Somaesthetics," 75–76.

29   Ibid., 77.

30   Ibid., 78.

31   Frantz Fanon, *Black Skin, White Masks* (New York: Grove Press, 1967), 109–40.

BIBLIOGRAPHY

Abani, Chris. *The Face: Cartography of the Void*. Brooklyn: Restless Books, 2013.

Ahmed, Sara. "Collective Feelings: Or, the Impressions Left by Others." *Theory, Culture & Society* 21, no. 2 (2004): 25–42. https://doi.org/10.1177/0263276404042133.

Ahmed, Sara. "Home and Away: Narratives of Migration and Estrangement." *International Journal of Cultural Studies* 2, no. 3 (1999): 329–47. https://doi.org/10.1177/136787799900200303.

Ahmed, Sara. *On Being Included: Racism and Diversity in Institutional Life*. Durham: Duke University, 2012.

Ahmed, Sara. "A Phenomenology of Whiteness." *Feminist Theory* 8, no. 2 (2008): 149–68. https://doi.org/10.1177/1464700107078139.

Ahmed, Sara and Jackie Stacey, *Thinking Through the Skin*. New York: Routledge, 2001.

Akinleye, Adesola. "Orientation for Communication: Embodiment, and the Language of Dance." *Empedocles: European Journal for the Philosophy of Communication* 4, no. 2 (2013): 101–12. https://doi.org/10.1386/ejpc.4.2.101_1.

Alcoff, Linda M. "The Phenomenology of Racial Embodiment." In Visible Identities: Race, Gender, and the Self, 179–95. New York: Oxford University Press, 2006.

Alcoff, Linda M. "Towards an Embodiment of Racial Phenomenology." *Radical Philosophy* 95 (1999): 15–26.

Alcoff, Linda M. *Visible Identities: Race, Gender and the Self*. Oxford: Oxford University Press, 2006.

Alexander, Bryant K. and John T. Warren. "The Materiality of Bodies: Critical Reflections on Pedagogy, Politics and Positionality." *Communication Quarterly* 50, no. 3–4 (2003): 328–43. https://doi.org/10.1080/01463370209385667.

Alim, Samy and Geneva Smitherman. *Articulate while Black: Barak Obama, Language, and Race in the U.S.* New York: Oxford University, 2012.

Al-Saji, Alia. "A Phenomenology of Hesitation: Interrupting Racializing Habits of Seeing." In *Living Alterities: Phenomenology, Embodiment, and Race*, edited by Emily S. Lee, 133–72. Albany: SUNY Press, 2014.

Andreescu, Florentina C. "Face and Facial Disfigurations: Self and Alterations of Self." *Psychotherapy and Politics International* 15, no. 2 (2017): 1–13. https://doi.org/10.1002/ppi.1407.

Austin, John Langshaw. *How to do Things with Words: Lecture II*, edited by James Opie Urmson and Marina Sbisá. Boston: Harvard University Press, 1962.

Avenanti, Alessio, Angela Sirigu, and Salvatore M. Aglioti. "Racial Bias Reduces Empathic Sensorimotor Resonance with Other-Race Pain." *Current Biology* 20 (2010): 1018–22. https://doi.org/10.1016/j.cub2010.03.071.

Baldwin, James. "If Black English Isn't a Language, Then Tell Me, What Is?" *The New York Times*, July 29, 1979. https://www.nytimes.com/books/98/03/29/specials/baldwin-english.html.

Beatty, Michael, James McCroskey, and Kory Floyd, eds. *Biological Dimensions of Communication: Perspectives, Research, and Methods.* Creskill: Hampton, 2009.

Bégin, Camilla. *Taste of the Nation: The New Deal Search for America's Food.* Urbana: University of Illinois Press, 2016.

Behnke, Elizabeth. "Interkinaesthetic Affectivity: A Phenomenological Approach." *Continental Philosophy Review* 41, no. 2 (2008): 143–61. https://doi.org/10.1007/s11007-008-9074-9.

Bergen, Benjamin. *Louder Than Words: The New Science of How the Mind Makes Meaning.* New York: Basic Books, 2012.

Berger, Martin. *Sight Unseen: Whiteness and American Visual Culture.* Berkeley: University of California Press, 2005.

Bhabha, Homi. *The Location of Culture.* New York: Routledge, 1994.

Black, Daniel. "What Is a Face?" *Body & Society* 17, no. 4 (2011): 1–25. https://doi.org/10.1177/1357034X11410450.

Blanke, Olaf. "Out of Body Experiences and Their Neural Basis: They are Linked to Multisensory and Cognitive Processing in the Brain." *British Medical Journal* 329, no. 7480 (2004): 1414–5. https://doi.org/10.1136/bmj.329.7480.1414.

Bochner, Arthur. "On First-Person Narrative Scholarship: Autoethnography as Acts of Meaning." *Narrative Inquiry* 22 (2012): 115–64.

Bonilla-Silva, Eduardo, Amanda Lewis, and David G. Embrick. "'I Did Not Get That Job Because of a Black Man...': The Story Lines and Testimonies of Color-Blind Racism." *Sociological Forum* 19, no. 4 (2004): 555–81. doi:10.1007/s11206-004-0696-3.

Bonilla-Silva, Eduardo, and Tyrone A. Forman. "'I Am not Racist but...': Mapping White College Students' Racial Ideology in the USA." *Discourse and Society* 11, no. 1 (2000): 50–85. doi: 10.1177/0957926500011001003.

Bourdieu, Pierre. *Outline of a Theory of Practice.* Cambridge: Cambridge University, 1977.

Bowen, Lisa Maria. "Reconfigured Bodies: The Problem of Ownership." *Communication Theory* 15, no. 1 (2005): 23–38. https://doi.org/10.1111/j.1468-2885.2005.tb00324.x.

Breggin, Peter R. "Empathic Self-Transformation and Love in Individual and Family Therapy." *Humanistic Psychologist* 27, no. 3 (1999): 267–82. https://doi.org/10.1080/08873267.1999.9986910.

Brown, Christopher. "Barack Obama as the Great Man: Communicative Constructions of Racial Transcendence in White-Male Elite Discourses." *Communication Monographs* 78, no. 4 (2011): 535–56. https://doi.org/10.1080/03637751.2011.618140.

Brown, Christopher. "Book Review: *Dog Whistle Politics: How Coded Racial Appeals Have Reinvented Racism and Wrecked the Middle Class.*" *Journalism and Mass Communication Quarterly* 92, no. 4 (2015): 1010–12. https://doi.org/10.1177/1077699015610327k.

Brown, Christopher. "Black Like Me, Black Like I Am! The Language and Memories of Race in Higher Education." In *Globalizing Intercultural Communication: A Reader,* edited by Kathryn Sorrells and Sachi Sekimoto, 115–21. Los Angeles: Sage, 2016.

Brunson, Rod. "Police Don't Like Black People: African-American Young Men's Accumulated Police Experiences." *Criminology and Public Policy* 6, no. 1 (2007): 71–102. https://doi.org/10.1111/j. 1745–9133.2007.00423.x.

Bull, Michael, Paul Gilroy, David Howes, and Douglas Kahn. "Introducing Sensory Studies." *The Senses and Society* 1, no. 1 (2006): 5–7. https://doi.org/10.2752/174589206778055655.

Butler, Judith. *Bodies that Matter: On the Discursive Limits of "Sex."* New York: Routledge, 1993.

Butler, Judith. "Endangered/Endangering: Schematic Racism and White Paranoia." In *Reading Rodney King, Reading Urban Uprising*, edited by Robert Gooding-Williams, 15–22. New York: Routledge, 1993.

Butler, Judith. "Performative Acts and Gender Constitution: An Essay in Phenomenology and Feminist Theory." *Theatre Journal* 40 (1988): 519–31.

Chawla, Devika, and Amardo Rodriguez. "Postcoloniality and the Speaking Body: Revisioning the English Oral Competency Curriculum." *Cultural Studies ←→ Critical Methodologies* 11, no. 1 (2011): 76–91. https://doi.org/10.1177/1532708610386923.

Ching, Leo. "Globalizing the Regional, Regionalizing the Global: Mass Culture and Asianism in the Age of Late Capital." *Public Culture* 12, no. 1 (2000): 233–57. https://doi.org/10.1215/08992363-12-1-233.

Classen, Constance. *The Deepest Touch: A Cultural History of Touch*. Urbana: University of Illinois Press, 2012.

Classen, Constance. "The Odor of the Other: Olfactory Symbolism and Cultural Categories." *Ethos* 20, no. 2 (1992): 133–66. https://doi.org/10.1525/eth.1992.20.2.02a00010.

Classen, Constance. "Speaking of Pain." In *the Book of Touch*, edited by Constance Classen, 109–14. New York: Berg, 2005.

Classen, Constance. *Worlds of Sense: Exploring the Senses in History and Across Cultures*. New York: Routledge, 1993.

Classen, Constance, David Howes, and Anthony Synnott. *Aroma: The Cultural History of Smell*. London: Routledge, 1994.

Coates, Ta-Nehisi. *Between the World and Me*. New York: Spiegel & Grau, 2015.

Cole, Jonathan. "Empathy Needs a Face." *Journal of Consciousness Studies* 8, no. 5–7 (2001): 51–68.

Csordas, Thomas J. "Somatic Mode of Attention." *Cultural Anthropology* 8, no. 2 (1993): 135–56.

de Beauvoir, Simone. *The Second Sex*. Translated by Constance Borde and Sheila Malovany-Chevallier. New York: Alfred A. Knope, 2010.

de Certeau, Michel. *Practice of Everyday Life*. Berkeley: University of California Press, 1988.

Deleuze, Gilles and Félix Guattari. *A Thousand Plateaus: Capitalism and Schizophrenia*. Translated by Brian Massumi. Minneapolis: University of Minnesota, 1987.

DiAngelo, Robin. *White Fragility: Why It Is So Hard for White People to Talk About Racism*. Boston: Beacon Press, 2018.

Diprose, Rosalyn. *Corporeal Generosity: On Giving with Nietzsche, Merleau-Ponty and Levinas*. Albany: State University of New York Press, 2002.

Dyson, Michael E. *Debating Race with Michael Eric Dyson*. Cambridge: Basic Civitas Books, 2007.

Eddo-Lodge, Reni. *Why I'm No Longer Talking to White People about Race*. London: Bloomsbury, 2017.

Ellis, Carolyn. *Revision: Autoethnographic Reflections on Life and Work*. Walnut Creek: Left Coast Press, 2009.

Fanon, Frantz. *Black Skins, White Masks*. Translated by Richard Philcox. New York: Grove Press, 2008.

Feagin, Joe R. "The Continuing Significance of Race: Anti-Black Discrimination in Public Places." *Sociological Review* 56, no. 1 (1991): 101–16.

Feagin, Joe R. The *White Racial Frame: Centuries of Racial Framing and Counter-Framing.* New York: Routledge, 2010.

Feagin, Joe R. and Eileen O'Brien. *White Men on Race: Power, Privilege, and the Shaping of a Cultural Consciousness.* Beacon: Beacon Press, 2003.

Ferranti, Michelle. "An Odor of Racism: Vaginal Deodorants in African-American Beauty Culture and Advertising." *Advertising & Society Review* 11, no. 4 (2011). http://muse.jhu.edu/journals/advertising_and_society_review/v011/11.4.ferranti.html.

Filmer, Alice Ashton. "Bilingual Belonging and the Whiteness of (Standard) English(es)." *Qualitative Inquiry* 13, no. 6 (2007): 747–65.

Foley, Megan. "'Prove You're Human': Fetishizing Material Embodiment and Immaterial Labor in Information Networks." *Critical Studies in Media Communication* 31, no. 5 (2014): 365–79. https://doi.org/10.1080/15295036.2014.939682.

Fordham, Signithia. "'Those Loud Black Girls': (Black) Women, Silence, and Gender 'Passing' in the Academy." *Anthropology and Education Quarterly* 24, no. 1 (1993): 3–32.

Frankenberg, Ruth. "'When We Are Capable of Stopping, We Begin to See': Being White, Seeing Whiteness." In *Names We Call Home: Autobiography on Racial Identity,* edited by Becky Thompson and Sangeeta Tyagi, 3–18. New York: Routledge, 1996.

Frankenberg, Ruth. *White Women, Race Matters: The Social Construction of Whiteness.* Minneapolis: University of Minnesota Press, 1993.

Friedman, Asia. "Perceptual Construction: Rereading the Social Construction of Reality through the Sociology of the Senses." *Cultural Sociology* 10, no. 1 (2016): 77–92. https://doi.org/10.1177/1749975515615149.

Friedman, Asia. "'There Are Two People at Work That I'm Fairly Certain Are Black': Uncertainty and Deliberative Thinking in Blind Race Attribution." *The Sociological Quarterly* 57, no. 3 (2016): 437–61. https://doi.org/10.1111/tsq.12140.

Friedman, Asia. "Toward a Sociology of Perception: Sight, Sex, and Gender." *Cultural Sociology* 5, no. 2 (2011): 187–206. https://doi.org/10.1177/1749975511400696.

Gates, Henry Louis. *The Signifying Monkey: A Theory of African American Literary Criticism.* Oxford: Oxford University Press, 1988.

Geurts, Kathryn Linn. "Consciousness as 'Feeling in the Body': A West African Theory of Embodiment, Emotion and the Making of Mind." In *Empire of the Senses: The Sensual Culture Reader,* edited by David Howes, 164–78. Oxford: Berg, 2005.

Geurts, Kathryn Linn. *Culture and the Senses: Bodily Ways of Knowing in an African Community.* Berkeley: University of California Press, 2002.

Granger, David A. "Somaesthetics and Racism: Toward an Embodied Pedagogy of Difference." *Journal of Aesthetic Education* 44, no. 3 (2010): 69–81. https://doi.org/10.1353/jae.2010.0000.

Grealy, Liam. "Negotiating Cultural Authenticity in Hip-Hop: Mimicry, Whiteness and Eminem." *Continuum: Journal of Media & Cultural Studies* 22, no. 6 (2008): 851–65. https://doi.org/10.1080/10304310802464821.

Griffin, Rachel Alicia. "Pushing Precious: Black Women, Media Representation, and the Glare of the White Supremacist Capitalist Patriarchal Gaze." *Critical Studies in Media Communication* 31, no. 3 (2014): 182–97. https://doi.org/10.1080/15295036.2013.849354.

Gumbrecht, Hans Ulrich and K. Ludwig Pfeiffer, eds. *Materialities of Communication.* Stanford: Stanford University Press, 1994.

Gustavo, Solomon. "Inside Black Lives Matter: The Very Hard Job of Becoming the Traveling Church of Civil Rights." *City Pages*, July 27, 2016. http://www.citypages.com/news/inside-black-lives-matter-the-very-hard-job-of-becoming-the-traveling-church-of-civil-rights/388277802.

Hacking, Ian. *The Social Construction of What?* Cambridge: Harvard University Press, 1999.

Haney López, Ian. *Dog Whistle Politics: How Coded Racial Appeals Have Reinvented Racism and Wrecked the Middle Class.* New York: Oxford University Press, 2014.

Hardcastle, William, John Laver, and Fiona Gibbon, eds. *The Handbook of Phonetic Sciences.* Malden: Blackwell, 2013.

Heidegger, Martin. *Being and Time.* Translated by John Macquarrie and Edward Robinson. New York: Harper and Row, 1962.

Hesse, Barnor. "Racialized Modernity: An Analytics of White Mythologies." *Ethnic and Racial Studies* 30, no. 4 (2007): 643–63. https://doi.org/10.1080/01419870701356064.

Ho, Pensri. "Performing the Oriental: Professionals and the Asian Model Minority Myth." *Journal of Asian American Studies* 6 (2003): 149–75. https://doi.org/10.1353/jaas.2004.0008.

Holman Jones, Stacy. "Autoethnography: Making the Personal Political." In *Handbook of Qualitative Research*, edited by Norman K. Denzin and Yvonna S. Lincoln, 63–91. Thousand Oaks: Sage, 2005.

Holmes, Malcolm and Brad Smith. *Race and Police Brutality: Roots of an Urban Dilemma.* Albany: SUNY Press, 2008.

hooks, bell. *Black Looks: Race and Representation.* Boston: South End Press, 1992.

hooks, bell. *Teaching to Transgress: Education as the Practice of Freedom.* New York: Routledge, 1994.

Howes, David. *Empire of the Senses: The Sensual Culture Reader.* Oxford: Berg, 2005.

Howes, David. "Introduction." In *Empire of the Senses: The Sensual Culture Reader*, edited by David Howes, 1–20. Oxford: Berg, 2005.

Howes, David. *Sensual Relations: Engaging the Senses in Culture and Social Theory.* Ann Arbor: University of Michigan Press, 2003.

Howes, David. "The Skinscape: Reflections on the Dermalogical Turn." *Body & Society* 24, no. 1–2 (2018): 225–39. https://doi.org/10.1177/1357034X18766285.

Howes, David and Constance Classen. *Ways of Sensing: Understanding the Senses in Society.* New York: Routledge, 2014.

Hudson, Nicky. "Towards Multi-Sensory Research: Acoustic Space, Racialisation and Whiteness." *Journal of Research in Nursing* 13, no. 2 (2008): 113–22. https://doi.org/10.1177/1744987108088663.

Hunter, Lisa and Elke Emerald. "Sensory Narratives: Capturing Embodiment in Narratives of Movement, Sport, Leisure, and Health." *Sport, Education, and Society* 21, no. 1 (2016): 28–46. https://doi.org/10.1080/13573322.2015.1065244.

Iwabuchi, Koichi. "Complicit Exoticism: Japan and Its Other." *Continuum* 8, no. 2 (1994): 49–82.

Jackson, Ronald L., and Heckman, Susan M. "Perceptions of White Identity and White Liability: An Analysis of White Student Responses to a College Campus Racial Hate Crime." *Journal of Communication* 52, no. 2 (2002): 434–50. https://doi.org/10.1111/j.1460-2466.2002.tb02554.x.

Johnson, Mark. *The Meaning of the Body: Aesthetics of Human Understanding.* Chicago: The University of Chicago Press, 2007.

Kawai, Yuko. "Stereotyping Asian Americans: The Dialectic of the Model Minority and the Yellow Peril." *Howard Journal of Communications* 16, no. 2 (2005): 109–30. https://doi-org.ezproxy.mnsu.edu/10.1080/10646170590948974.

Kim, David Haekwon. "Shame and Self-Revision in Asian American Assimilation." In *Living Alterities: Phenomenology, Embodiment, and Race*, edited by Emily S. Lee, 103–32. Albany: SUNY Press, 2014.

Kim, Janine Young. "Racial Emotions and the Feeling of Equality." *University of Colorado Law Review* 87 (2016): 438–96.

Kirk, David and Andrew Papachristos, "Cultural Mechanisms and the Persistence of Neighborhood." *American Journal of Sociology* 11, no. 4 (2011): 1190–233. http://www.jstor.org/stable/10.1086/655754.

Kittler, Friedrich. *Discourse Networks 1800/1900*. Translated by Michael Metter and Chris Cullens. Stanford: Stanford University Press, 1990.

Kraidy, Marwan. "Hybridity in Cultural Globalization." *Communication Theory* 12, no. 3 (2002): 316–39.

Ku, Robert Ji-Song. *Dubious Gastronomy: The Cultural Politics of Eating Asian in the USA*. Honolulu: University of Hawaii Press, 2014.

Kuhn, Timothy, ed. *Matters of Communication: Political, Cultural and Technological Challenges*. New York: Hampton Press, 2011.

Küpers, Wendelin. "'Inter-communicating': Phenomenological Perspectives on Embodied Communication and Contextuality." *Journal for Communication & Culture* 2 (2012): 114–38.

Lafrance, Marc. "Skin and the Self: Cultural Theory and Anglo-American Psychoanalysis." *Body & Society* 15, no. 3 (2009): 3–24. https://doi.org/10.1177/1357034X09339099.

Lakoff, George and Mark Johnson. *Metaphors We Live By*. Chicago: University of Chicago Press, 1980.

Lakoff, George and Mark Johnson. *Philosophy in the Flesh: The Embodied Mind and Its Challenge to Western Thought*. New York: Basic Books, 1999.

Langellier, Kristin M. and Eric E. Peterson *Performing Narrative: Storytelling in Daily Life*. Philadelphia: Temple University Press, 2011.

Largey, Gale Peter and David Rodney Watson. "The Sociology of Odors." *American Journal of Sociology* 77, no. 6 (1972): 1021–34. https://www.jstor.org/stable/2776218.

Le Breton, David. *Sensing the World: An Anthropology of the Senses*. Translated by Carmen Ruschiensky. London: Bloomsbury Academic, 2017.

Lee, Felicia. "Lingering Conflict in the Schools: Black Dialect vs. Standard Speech." *The New York Times*, January 5, 1994. https://www.nytimes.com/1994/01/05/nyregion/lingering-conflict-in-the-schools-black-dialect-vs-standard-speech.html.

Lee, Emily S. "The Epistemology of the Question of Authenticity, in Place of Strategic Essentialism." *Hypatia: A Journal of Feminist Philosophy* 26, no. 2 (2011): 258–79.

Lee, Emily S., ed. *Living Alterities: Phenomenology, Embodiment, and Race*. Albany: SUNY Press, 2014.

Lee, Kyoo. "Why Asian Female Stereotypes Matter to All: Beyond Black and White, East and West." *Critical Philosophy of Race* 1, no. 1 (2013): 86–103.

Lei, Joy. "(Un)necessary Toughness?: Those 'Loud Black Girls' and Those 'Quiet Asian Boys.'" *Anthropology & Education Quarterly* 34, no. 2 (2003): 158–81. https://doi.org/10.1525/aeq.2003.34.2.158.

Leonardo, Zeus and Michalinos Zembylas. "Whiteness as Technology of Affect: Implications for Educational Praxis." *Equity and Excellence in Education* 46, no. 1 (2013): 150–65. https://doi.org/10.1080/10665684.2013.750539.

Lim, Jason. "Immanent Politics: Thinking Race and Ethnicity through Affect and Machinism." *Environment and Planning A* 42 (2010): 2392–409. https://doi.org/doi:10.1068/a42234.

Lipsitz, George. *The Possessive Investment in Whiteness: How White People Profit From Identity Politics.* Philadelphia, Temple University Press, 2006.

Low, Kelvin E. Y. "Olfactive Frames of Remembering: Theorizing Self, Senses and Society." *The Sociological Review* 61, no. 4 (2013): 688–708. https://doi.org/10.1111/1467-954X.12078.

Low, Kelvin E. Y. *Scent and Scent-sibilities: Smell and Everyday Life Experiences.* Newcastle-upon-Tyne: Cambridge Scholars Publishing, 2009.

Lund, Katrín. "Seeing in Motion and the Touching Eye: Walking over Scotland's Mountain." *Etnofoor* 18, no. 1 (2005): 27–42. http://www.jstor.org/stable/25758084.

Macedo, Donaldo, Bessie Dendrinos, and Panayota Gounari. *The Hegemony of English.* Boulder: Paradigm Publishers, 2003.

Manalansan, Martin F. IV. "Immigrant Lives and the Politics of Olfaction in the Global City." In *The Smell Culture Reader*, edited by Jim Drobnick, 41–52. Oxford: Berg, 2006.

Mann, Geoff. "Why Does Country Music Sound White? Race and the Voice of Nostalgia." *Ethnic and Racial Studies* 31, no. 1 (2008): 73–100. https://doi.org/10.1080/01419870701538893.

Manning, Erin. *Politics of Touch: Space, Movement, Sovereignty.* Minneapolis: University of Minnesota Press, 2007.

Marks, Laura U. *The Skin of the Film: Intercultural Cinema, Embodiment, and the Senses.* Durham: Duke University Press, 2000.

Martin, Judith N., Robert L. Krizek, Thomas K. Nakayama, and Lisa Bradford. "What Do White People Want to Be Called? A Study of Self-labels for White Americans." In *Whiteness: The Communication of Social Identity*, edited by Thomas K. Nakayama and Judith N. Martin, 27–50. Thousand Oaks: Sage, 1999.

Martinez, Jacqueline. *Phenomenology of Chicana Experience and Identity: Communication and Transformation in Praxis.* Lanham: Rowman & Littlefield, 2000.

Marx, Karl. *Economic and Philosophic Manuscripts of 1844.* Translated by Martin Milligan. New York: International Publishers, 1964.

Massumi, Brian. *Parables for the Virtual: Movement, Affect, Sensation.* Durham: Duke University Press, 2002.

McIntosh, Peggy. "White Privilege: Unpacking the Invisible Knapsack." In *Race, Class, and Gender in the United States, 6th edition: An Integrated Study*, edited by Paula Rothenberg, 188–92. New York: Worth Publishers, 2004.

McLaren, Peter. *Schooling as a Ritual Performance: Towards a Political Economy of Education Symbols and Gestures.* New York: Routledge, 1986.

McLuhan, Marshall *Understanding Media.* New York: McGraw-Hill, 1964.

McWhorter, John. "The Perpetual Failure to Understand Obama's Double Consciousness." *New Republic*, October 3, 2012. http://www.newrepublic.com/article/108180/perpetual-failure-understand-obamas-double-consciousness.

Merleau-Ponty, Maurice. *Phenomenology of Perception*. Translated by Colin Smith. London: Routledge and Kegan Paul, 1962.

Mills, Charles. *The Racial Contract*. Ithaca: Cornell University Press, 1997.

Moon, Dreama. "White Enculturation and Bourgeois Ideology: The Discursive Production of 'Good White Girls.'" In *Whiteness: The Communication of Social Identity*, edited by Thomas K. Nakayama and Judith N. Martin, 177–97. Thousand Oaks: Sage, 1999.

Moreira, Claudio and Marcelo Diversi. "Missing Bodies: Troubling the Colonial Landscape of American Academia." *Text and Performance Quarterly* 31, no. 3 (2011): 229–48. https://doi-org.ezproxy.mnsu.edu/10.1080/10462937.2011.573190.

Morris, David. *The Culture of Pain*. Los Angeles: University of California, 1991.

Myers, Kristen A. and Passion Williamson. "Race Talk: The Perpetuation of Racism through Private Discourse." *Race and Society* 4, no. 1 (2001): 3–26. https://doi.org/10.1016/S1090-9524(02)00032-3.

Nandy, Ashis. "Ethnic Cuisine: The Significant 'Other.'" *India International Centre Quarterly* 29, no. 3 (2003): 246–51.

Newell, Fiona and Ladan Shams. "New Insights into Multisensory Perception." *Perception* 36 (2007): 1415–17. https://doi.org/10.1068/p3610ed.

Ngo, Helen. *The Habits of Racism: A Phenomenology of Racism and Racialized Embodiment*. Lanham: Lexington Books, 2017.

Ngo, Helen. "Racist Habits: A Phenomenological Analysis of Racism and the Habitual Body." *Philosophy & Social Criticism* 42, no. 9 (2016): 847–72. https://doi.org/10.1177/0191453715623320.

Obasogie, Osagie K. *Blinded by Sight: Seeing Race Through the Eyes of the Blind*. Stanford: Stanford University Press, 2014.

Obasogie, Osagie K. "Do Blind People See Race? Social, Legal, and Theoretical Considerations." *Law & Society Review* 44, no. 3 (2010): 585–616. https://doi.org/10.1111/j.1540-5893.2010.00417.x.

Ozeki, Ruth. *The Face: A Time Code*. Brooklyn: Restless Books, 2015.

Pagis, Michal. "Embodied Self-reflexivity." *Social Psychology Quarterly* 72, no. 3 (2009): 265–83. https://doi.org/10.1177/019027250907200308.

Perry, Pamela. "White Universal Identity as a 'Sense of Group Position.'" *Symbolic Interaction* 30, no. 3 (2007): 375–93. doi: 10.1525/si.2007.30.3.375.

Petherbridge, Danielle. "Racializing Perception and the Phenomenology of Invisibility." In *Body/Self/Other: The Phenomenology of Social Encounters*, edited by Luna Dolezal and Danielle Petherbridge, 103–29. Albany: SUNY Press, 2017.

Pink, Sarah. *Doing Sensory Ethnography*. London: Sage, 2009.

Poole, Deborah. *Vision, Race, and Modernity: A Visual Economy of the Andean World*. Princeton: Princeton University, 1997.

Puar, Jasbir. "'I Would Rather Be a Cyborg than a Goddess': Becoming-Intersectional in Assemblage Theory." *philoSOPHIA* 2, no. 1 (2012): 49–66.

Puar, Jasbir. *Terrorist Assemblages: Homonationalism in Queer Times*. Durham: Duke University, 2007.

Rhys-Taylor, Alex. "Disgust and Distinction: The Case of the Jellied Eel." *The Sociological Review* 61 (2013): 227–46. https://doi.org/10.1111/1467-954X.12015.

Rhys-Taylor, Alex. *Food and Multiculture: A Sensory Ethnography of East London*. London: Bloomsbury Academic, 2017.

Rogers, Carl. "Empathic: An Unappreciated Way of Being." *Counseling Psychologist* 5, no. 2, (1975): 2–10. https://doi.org/10.1177/001100007500500202.

Rosan, Peter J. "The Poetics of Intersubjective Life: Empathy and the Other." *The Humanistic Psychologist* 40, no. 2 (2012): 115–35. https://doi.org/10.1080/08873267.2012.643685.

Rosenbaum, Dennis, Amie M. Schuck, Sandra K. Costello, Darnell F. Hawkins, and Marianne K. Ring. "Attitudes toward the Police: The Effects of Direct and Vicarious Experience." *Police Quarterly* 8, no. 3 (2005): 343–65. https://doi.org/10.1177/1098611104271085.

Rutter, Jon D. "Dismantling the Face: Toward a Phenomenology of Boxing." *Cultural Studies ↔ Critical Methodologies* 7, no. 3 (2007): 281–93. https://doi.org/10.1177/1532708606297159.

Sacks, Oliver. *A Leg to Stand on*. New York: Touchstone, 1998.

Saldanha, Arun. *Psychedelic White: Goa Trance and the Viscosity of Race*. Minneapolis: University of Minnesota, 2007.

Saldanha, Arun. "Reontologizing Race: The Machinic Geography of Phenotype." *Environment and Planning D: Society and Space* 24 (2006): 9–24. https://doi.org/10.1068/d61j.

Scarry, Elaine. *The Body in Pain: The Making and Unmaking of the World*. New York: Oxford University, 1985.

Schlichter, Annette. "Do Voices Matter? Vocality, Materiality, Gender Performativity." *Body & Society* 17, no. 1 (2011): 31–52. https://doi.org/10.1177/1357034X10394669.

Sekimoto, Sachi. "'Materiality of the Self' Toward a Reconceptualization of Identity in Communication." In *Matters of Communication: Political, Cultural, and Technological Challenges to Communication Theorizing*, edited by Timothy Kuhn, 47–64. New York: Hampton Press, 2011.

Sekimoto, Sachi. "A Multimodal Approach to Identity; Theorizing the Self through Embodiment, Spatiality, and Temporality." *Journal of International and Intercultural Communication* 5, no. 3 (2012): 226–43. https://doi.org/10.1080/17513057.2012.689314.

Sekimoto, Sachi. "Race and the Senses: Toward Articulating the Sensory Apparatus of Race." *Critical Philosophy of Race* 6, no. 1 (2018): 82–100. https://doi.org/10.5325/critphilrace.6.1.0082.

Sekimoto, Sachi. "Transnational Asia: Dis/orienting Identity in the Globalized World." *Communication Quarterly* 62, no. 4 (2014): 381–98. http://dx.doi.org/10.1080/01463373.2014.922485.

Serres, Michel. *The Five Senses: A Philosophy of Mingled Bodies*. Translated by Margaret Sankey and Peter Cowley. London: Bloomsbury Academic, 2016.

Sheets-Johnstone, Maxine. *The Primacy of Movement*. Philadelphia: John Benjamins Publishing Company, 1999.

Shotwell, Alexis. *Knowing Otherwise: Race, Gender, and Implicit Understanding*. University Park: The Pennsylvania State University Press, 2011.

Shusterman, Richard. *Body Consciousness: A Philosophy of Mindfulness and Somaesthetics*. Cambridge: Cambridge University Press, 2008.

Shusterman, Richard. "Somaesthetics and the Body/Media Issue." *Body & Society* 3, no. 3 (1997): 33–49. https://doi.org/10.1177/1357034X97003003002.

Slaby, Jan. "Affective Intentionality and the Feeling Body." *Phenomenology and the Cognitive Sciences* 7, no. 4 (2008): 429–44. https://doi.org/10.1007/s11097-007-9083-x.

Smith, Mark. *How Race Is Made: Slavery, Segregation, and the Senses.* Chapel Hill: University of North Carolina Press, 2006.

Sparkes, Andrew C. "Ethnography and the Senses: Challenges and Possibilities." *Qualitative Research in Sport and Exercise* 1, no. 1 (2009): 30–31. https://doi.org/10.1080/ 19398440802567923.

Spronk, Rachel. "Sexuality and Subjectivity: Erotic Practices and the Question of Bodily Sensations." *Social Anthropology* 22, no. 1 (2014): 3–21. https://doi.org/10.1111/ 1469-8676.12055.

Spronk, Rachel and Christian Klaufus. "Introduction: Taste." *Etnofoor* 24, no. 2 (2012): 7–11. https://www.jstor.org/stable/43264043.

Stawarska, Beata. "Mutual Gaze and Social Cognition." *Phenomenology and the Cognitive Sciences* 5, no. 1 (2006): 17–30. https://doi.org/10.1007/s11097-005-9009-4.

Stawarska, Beata. "Seeing Faces: Sartre and Imitation Studies." *Sartre Studies International* 13, no. 2 (2007): 27–46. https://doi.org/10.3167/ssi.2007/130202.

Stein, Edith Stein. *On the Problem of Empathy.* Translated by Waltraut Stein. Washington DC: Institute of Carmelite Studies Publications, 1989.

Stoever, Jennifer Lynn. "Fine-tuning the Sonic Color-line: Radio and the Acousmatic Du Bois." *Modernist Cultures* 10, no. 1 (2015): 99–118.

Stoever, Jennifer Lynn. *The Sonic Color Line: Race and the Cultural Politics of Listening.* New York: New York University Press, 2016.

Stoller, Paul. *Sensuous Scholarship.* Philadelphia: University of Pennsylvania Press, 1997.

Sullivan, Shannon. "The Hearts and Guts of White People: Ethics, Ignorance, and the Physiology of White Racism." *Journal of Religious Ethics* 42, no. 4 (2014): 591–611. https://doi.org/10.1111/jore.12074.

Sullivan, Shannon. *The Physiology of Sexist and Racist Oppression.* Oxford: Oxford University Press, 2015.

Sullivan, Shannon. *Revealing Whiteness: The Unconscious Habits of Racial Privilege.* Bloomington: Indiana University, 2004.

Sun, Ge. "How Does Asia mean? (Part I)." *Inter-Asia Cultural Studies* 1, no. 1 (2000): 13–47.

Sun, Ge. "How Does Asia mean? (Part II)." *Inter-Asia Cultural Studies* 1, no. 2 (2000): 319–41. Sutton, David. "Food and the Senses." *Annual Review of Anthropology* 39 (2010): 209–23. https: doi.org/10.1146/annurev.anthro.012809.104957.

Swanton, Dan. "Sorting Bodies: Race, Affect, and Everyday Multiculture in a Mill Town in Northern England." *Environment and Planning A* 42, no. 10 (2010): 2332–50. https:// doi.org/ 10.1068/a42395.

Synnott, Anthony. "Puzzling Over the Senses: From Plato to Marx." In *The Varieties of Sensory Experience. A Source Book in the Anthropology of the Senses*, edited by David Howes, 71–6. Toronto: University of Toronto, 1991.

Tamari, Tomoko. "The Phenomenology of Architecture: A Short Introduction to Juhani Pallasmaa." *Body & Society* 23, no. 1 (2017): 91–5. https://doi.org/10.1177/135703 4X16676540.

Tankei-Aminian, Sachiko. "On Becoming Japersican: A Personal Narrative of Cultural Adaptation, Intercultural Identity, and Transnationalism." In *Globalizing Intercultural Communication: A Reader*, edited by Kathryn Sorrells and Sachi Sekimoto, 197–205. Thousand Oaks, CA: Sage, 2016.

Terrill, William and Michael Reisig. "Neighborhood Context and Police Use of Force." *Journal of Research on Crime and Delinquency* 40, no. 3 (2003): 291–321. https://doi.org/10.1177/0022427803253800.

Tsuda, Yukio. "Speaking against the Hegemony of English: Problems, Ideologies, and Solutions." In *The Handbook of Critical Intercultural Communication*, edited by Thomas K. Nakayama and Rona T. Halualani, 248–69. Malden, MA: Wiley-Blackwell, 2010.

Tyler, Tom and Cheryl J. Wakslak. "Profiling and Police Legitimacy: Procedural Justice, Attributions of Motive, and Acceptance of Police Authority." *Criminology* 42, no. 2 (2004): 253–82. https://doi.org/10.1111/j.1745-9125.2004.tb00520.x.

Vannini, Phillip, Dennis Waskul, and Simon Gottschalk. *The Senses in Self, Society, and Culture: A Sociology of the Senses*. New York: Routledge, 2012.

Vasterling, Veronica. "Body and Language: Butler, Merleau-Ponty and Lyotard on the Speaking Embodied Subject." *International Journal of Philosophical Studies* 11, no. 2 (2003): 205–23. https://doi.org/10.1080/0967255032000074190.

Waitt, Gordon. "Bodies that Sweat: The Affective Responses of Young Women in Wollongong, New South Wales, Australia." *Gender, Place and Culture* 21, no. 6 (2014): 666–82. https://doi.org/10.1080/0966369X.2013.802668.

Walmsley, Emily. "Race, Place and Taste: Making Identities through Sensory Experience in Ecuador." *Etnofoor* 18, no. 1 (2005): 43–60.

Wang, Yiman. "Screening Asia: Passing, Performative Translation, and Reconfiguration." *Positions* 15, no. 2 (2007): 319–43. https://doi.org/10.1215/10679847-2006-037.

Warren, John T. and Amy Kilgard. "Staging Stain upon the Snow: Performance as a Critical Enfleshment of Whiteness." *Text and Performance Quarterly* 21 (2001): 261–76. https://doi.org/10.1080/10462930128129.

Washida, Kiyokazu. 鷲田清一. *Kao no Genshōgaku* 顔の現象学 [Phenomenology of the Face]. Tokyo: Kōdansha, 1996.

Waskul, Dennis, Phillip Vannini, Janelle Wilson. "The Aroma of Recollection: Olfaction, Nostalgia, and the Shaping of the Sensuous Self." *The Senses and Society* 4, no. 1 (2009): 5–22. https://doi.org/10.2752/174589309X388546.

Weiss, Gail. "Sedimented Attitudes and Existential Responsibilities." In *Body/Self/Other: The Phenomenology of Social Encounters*, edited by Luna Dolezal and Danielle Petherbridge, 75–102. Albany: SUNY Press, 2017.

Weitzer, Ronald. "Racialized Policing: Residents' Perceptions in Three Neighborhoods." *Law & Society Review* 34, no. 1 (2000): 129–55. https://doi.org/10.2307/3115118.

Wiegman, Robyn. "Whiteness Studies and the Paradox of Particularity." *Boundary* 26, no. 3 (1999): 115–50.

Wise, Amanda and Adam Chapman. "Introduction: Migration, Affect, and the Senses." *Journal of Intercultural Studies*, 26, no. 1–2 (2005): 1–3. https://doi.org/10.1080/07256860500074425.

Wise, Tim. *White Like Me: Reflections on Race from a Privileged Son*. Brooklyn: Soft Skull, 2008.

Xu, Xiaojing, Xiangyu Zuo, Xiaoying Wang, and Shihui Han. "Do You Feel My Pain? Racial Group Membership Modulates Empathic Neural Responses." *The Journal of Neuroscience* 29, no. 26 (2009): 8525–9. https://doi.org/10.1523/JNEUROSCI.2418-09.2009.

Yancy, George. *Black Bodies, White Gazes: The Continuing Significance of Race*. Lanham: Rowman and Littlefield, 2008.

Yancy, George. *Look, a White!: Philosophical Essays on Whiteness*. Philadelphia: Temple University Press, 2012.

Yep, Gust. "Queering/Quaring/Kauering/Crippin'/Transing 'Other Bodies' in Intercultural Communication." *Journal of International and Intercultural Communication* 6, no. 2 (2013): 118–26. https://doi.org/10.1080/17513057.2013.777087.

Young, Iris Marion. *On Female Body Experience: "Throwing Like a Girl" and Other Essays*. New York: Oxford University, 2005.

Young, Iris Marion. "Throwing Like a Girl: A Phenomenology of Feminine Body Comportment, Motility, and Spatiality." In *Identities: Race, Class, Gender, and Nationality*, edited by Linda M. Alcoff and Eduardo Mendieta, 163–74. Oxford: Blackwell, 2003.

Zembylas, Michalinos. "Rethinking Race and Racism as *Technologies of Affect*: Theorizing the Implications for Anti-racist Politics and Practice in Education." *Race Ethnicity and Education* 18, no. 2 (2015): 145–62. https://doi.org/ 10.1080/13613324.2014.946492.

INDEX